17⁵⁰

Patricia Anne Norton
74 Cliff St
Naugatuck
Con

AND THERE STANDING ON THE TOE OF JOANNE'S MOC-
CASIN WAS THE MOST WONDERFUL AND BEAUTIFUL
THING THAT JOANNE COULD POSSIBLY IMAGINE

A Little Maid
of
Mohawk Valley

BY
ALICE TURNER CURTIS

Author of
"The Little Maid Historical Books," "Yankee Girls Civil War Stories"

Illustrated by
GRACE NORCROSS

THE PENN PUBLISHING
COMPANY PHILADELPHIA

INTRODUCTION

LITTLE Joanne Clarke, who once saw a fairy, lived with her father and mother in a big log cabin in the Mohawk Valley. In May, 1777, she and her friend, Nancy Wagner, were taken captives by an Indian, one of the allies of the British who were then waging war against American Liberties. The Indian disappears, leaving the little girls alone in the depths of the forest; they discover his pouch, that contains a letter to an English general with information valuable to the American Army at Albany, and Joanne carries the pouch to General Philip Schuyler.

Many adventures befall her before she again reaches her home in safety. She was at the besieged Fort Stanwix when brave Herkimer fell at Oriskany and the little maid of Mohawk Valley helped to make the first regulation American flag that ever floated over an American fort.

CONTENTS

ILLUSTRATIONS

A Little Maid of Mohawk Valley

CHAPTER I

A CANOE TRIP

"MOTHER! This is the morning that you promised we would go for a day's visit with the Wagners. You said: 'If 'tis pleasant on Tuesday we will surely go!' and now it is pleasant and it is Tuesday. And may I not wear my open-work white stockings? May I not, Mother dear? It is as warm as summer, truly it is!" and Joanne clasped both hands about her mother's arm and looked up pleadingly into Mrs. Clarke's smiling face.

"Joanne! Be careful! I came near spilling the meal, and meal is not easily come by now that the British and Indian soldiers are seizing provisions everywhere from loyal Americans," said Mrs. Clarke, turning from the kitchen table, and glancing out through the open doorway as if to make sure that the May morning was as pleasant as her little daughter declared. "It is indeed

9

good weather for the season," she continued thoughtfully.

"Oh, Mother! The wild cherry is in bloom," and Joanne drew her mother toward the open door and out on the rough porch of the log cabin. "Look!" and the little girl pointed toward the valley that seemed filled with a white drift of blossoms. From where they stood they could look for miles up the beautiful valley of the Mohawk, stretched out like a huge map, with its calm river, high bluffs, and in the distance the blue haze of the Green Mountains.

"It will be a fine day for our visit," said Mrs. Clarke, "but you'd best not think of white stockings. It is full likely we may have rough walking; and, beside that, Joanne, I fear the little Wagner girls have nothing as fine as your open-work stockings and it is never good manners to dress better than those with whom you consort."

"I did but wish to show them to Nancy and Lucy," Joanne explained. "And are we not to go in the canoe, Mother? 'Tis a much easier way, and I could paddle! Let us go in the canoe, Mother dear!" and Joanne hopped up and down in her eagerness to win her mother's consent to her plan.

"Very well. We will go in the canoe, and we will be off at once before the morning grows late. Run and get your sunbonnet, and I will pack a small basket. There is a good stock of jam in my storeroom, and I doubt not Mrs. Wagner will welcome a few jars," and Mrs. Clarke turned back to the big kitchen whose huge fireplace and brick oven nearly filled one end of the room. She took a covered basket from a corner shelf and opened a door leading into a storeroom where the household supplies were kept, while Joanne took her sunbonnet of pink checked gingham from its hook near the door and declared herself all ready to start, and in a few moments Mrs. Clarke stepped from the storeroom with the well-filled basket.

"Close the back door, Joanne, and set the bar in place, and the window-shutters also. Your father will not be back from Schenectady before sunset, and 'tis best the house be fastened," and as she spoke Mrs. Clarke set down the basket, took up a long-handled fire-shovel and began covering the glowing coals in the broad fireplace with ashes: this would keep the heat and fire alive until their return.

Meanwhile Joanne had lifted the heavy bar

into the firm holders on each side of the door, closed the window-shutters and was again on the porch eager to start on the day's visit.

Joanne had just passed her tenth birthday. She was rather tall for a girl of ten, and very straight and active. Her gray eyes were clear and fearless, and her brown hair waved back from her forehead into a solid braid that nearly reached her waist. There were many freckles on her straight little nose and brown cheeks, for Joanne was out of doors almost as much as a young Indian girl. In the spring days she helped her father plant the vegetable garden on the southern slope in front of the house, and cared for the honeysuckle and climbing rose vines that grew about the cabin, planted such flower seeds as she could secure in the round bed at the corner of the house, and brought home flowering plants from the fields and woods.

When the first strawberries were ripe Joanne knew just where to find them, and brought home well-filled baskets of the delicious berries for her mother to make into jam, when sugar could be secured, or to dry and keep for winter use. Later on blueberries, raspberries, blackberries, and other wild fruits were gathered, and in au-

tumn hazelnuts, beechnuts, chestnuts and walnuts were plenty, and were stored away to help
out the winter needs.

Joanne could swim, her father declared, " as
well as any boy in Tryon County," and Mr.
Clarke had taught her to paddle a canoe, and
she knew many a stream where she could catch
a mess of trout for the midday meal. She knew
the name and song of many of the wild birds that
filled the woodland and valley with their music,
for in 1777 the Mohawk Valley was not only the
home of many birds, but elk and deer were found
there in great numbers, as were foxes, beavers,
wolves and bears. The settlers, like Joanne's father and mother, had to depend wholly upon
themselves for all their needs, and children were
early taught to be useful indoors and out.

" Nancy and Lucy will be looking out for us.
I am sure they will," said Joanne happily, as she
walked beside her mother down the path that led
from the clearing about the cabin toward the
river. " Nancy said that when May came she
and Lucy would watch for us every pleasant
morning. And I have a present for each of
them," she added, with a smiling nod as her
mother looked at her questioningly.

"Presents? Where are they? They must be in your pocket, for I see no basket or bundle," responded Mrs. Clarke, and again Joanne nodded. She thought it great fun to puzzle her mother, and said:

"Wait and see, Mother dear! But I truly have a gift for Nancy and one for Lucy. But I do wish I might have worn my Sunday dress, and the open-work stockings that Grandma Clarke sent me from Albany," and Joanne's smile vanished as she looked down at her worn moccasins, and the skirt of brown linsey-woolsey that came nearly to her ankles.

"But why do you think so much of being fine to-day, Joanne? This is not your first visit to the little Wagner girls. 'Tis but a fortnight ago your father took you, and you went happily enough in your every-day garments." And Mrs. Clarke looked at her little daughter, wondering why Joanne, who seldom thought of what she wore, should again speak of the fine stockings from Albany.

Joanne's face was now sober, and she made no response. They had reached the little sandy cove, overhung by wide-spreading beech trees, where the birch-bark canoe was drawn up, and

Joanne ran to get the paddles that were hidden in the underbrush near by, while her mother drew the light craft to the water's edge, put the basket in, and in a few moments Joanne, kneeling in the bow, was skilfully paddling the canoe upstream toward the Wagners' home.

" Keep well in the shadow of the trees along the shore," cautioned Mrs. Clarke, and Joanne nodded, for the little girl as well as her mother knew that a terrible danger threatened all loyal Americans who had made their home in the beautiful Mohawk Valley. The English Crown and the Tories living in America did not, in the terrible struggle of 1777, hesitate to use the Indians to help conquer the American effort for independence, and the Mohawks now prowled woods and streams, sometimes taking captives or destroying homes, and bringing fear and suffering to all; and Joanne as well as her mother knew this, and she now dipped her paddle cautiously, and the canoe slipped through the water silently. Well in the shadow of the overhanging trees both Mrs. Clarke and Joanne felt sure that larger canoes passing in mid-channel would not notice the little craft that crept so silently along the shore.

Joanne, however, soon forgot the possibility of danger as she thought of the pleasures of a day's visit with Nancy and Lucy Wagner, the only girl playmates she had ever had. Nancy was nearly twelve, while Lucy was two years younger than Joanne. They were neither of them as strong as Joanne, and even the twelve-year-old Nancy was, as a rule, ready to agree to whatever plan Joanne had for games or amusement of any kind; while Lucy was quite sure that whatever Nancy and Joanne decided on was absolutely right, and the three little girls usually played together happily. This morning Joanne was thinking of the delight of her friends when she should give them the presents that now rested securely in the deep pocket of her brown skirt. On the previous day, playing on the sandy shore of the river, Joanne had discovered a treasure store of tiny mussel shells, and these she had promptly gathered and taken to her playhouse, a small cave-like opening that ran in to the side of a high bluff just beyond the sandy stretch of shore.

In this playhouse Joanne kept many treasures: there was a small stump with a smooth top that made an excellent seat: Joanne had tugged the stump up the bluff from the shore, and she had also carpeted the floor of the cave with a soft green moss that she had brought from the woods. Here she kept a family of dolls made from corn-cobs, and dressed in whatever materials she could secure. In one corner was a huge hornet's nest; her father had smoked the hornets out and Joanne had eagerly claimed it.

To the cave she had carried the tiny shells, and with the aid of a darning-needle she had succeeded in piercing and stringing them into necklaces. These, carefully wrapped in the soft inner bark of a silver birch tree, were now in her pocket, and as the canoe crept into a creek that would lead to the landing-place near the Wagners' home, Joanne resolved to show the necklaces to her mother as soon as they reached the shore.

Just as the canoe reached the shore a sudden exclamation from her mother made Joanne look over her shoulder.

" What is it, Mother? " she asked.

" Indians! " Mrs. Clarke replied in a whisper. " Look up the path, Joanne. There are four of them, and they are going straight toward the Wagners' cabin! What shall we do! It may

even be Brant himself!" and putting her arm
about Joanne Mrs. Clarke quickly drew the little
girl behind a thick growth of underbrush, where
they crouched without even a whispered word,
peering through an opening until sure the red
men had not discovered them.

CHAPTER II

JOANNE AND THE INDIANS

"PERHAPS these are friendly Mohawks," said Joanne. "May I not creep through the woods to the cabin and find out? My moccasins will not make any noise, and I will not even break a twig."

For a moment Mrs. Clarke did not reply. She was thinking of the Mohawk chief, "Thayen-dangea," who, since being sent to school by a generous Englishman, and educated as a white boy, was known as Joseph Brant, and who now headed the Mohawks, the allies of the British, against the Americans who were fighting for the independence of their country.

Joanne's suggestion, however, that the Indians they had seen moving toward the Wagners' cabin might, after all, be on some friendly errand, gave her mother new courage. She knew that her little daughter could go as swiftly and silently as any Indian, and she now resolved to go with her.

But to this Joanne objected.

19

" You cannot walk as softly as I can. Let me go alone; please let me, Mother. And you return to the canoe and wait for me there. I'll come straight back as soon as I find out the Indians' errand," and before Mrs. Clarke could answer Joanne had slipped away into the woods, and even in the great danger that seemed so near Mrs. Clarke could but smile at the thought of her little daughter's courage.

" Joanne knows not fear, and perhaps 'tis better so," she thought as she crept down to the canoe. She felt sure that Joanne was in no greater danger than when hiding in the underbrush, and resolved to wait her return with all the courage she could summon.

Joanne was now glad indeed that she had on the old moccasins instead of the white stockings and leather slippers that she had wanted to wear. She ran lightly over the woodland moss, turning from the path now and then to stop and listen, a little fearfully, for any sound from the cabin.

But the woods were still except for a little murmuring breeze that drifted over the tree-tops, and the springtime songs of birds, and in a few moments Joanne was at the edge of the clearing in which stood the Wagners' cabin.

Standing behind a big chestnut tree the little girl looked anxiously toward the cabin, and in a moment she drew a long breath and was no longer afraid, for she could see that one of the Indians was sitting on the porch step while Lucy Wagner stood close beside him. Behind them she could see Nancy and Mrs. Wagner bringing food to the three other Indians.

" Oh, goody! goody!" whispered Joanne, tempted to run forward and join her friends. But she turned and sped back to the river, and from the canoe her mother came hurrying to meet her.

" They are friendly Mohawks, I am sure they are, Mother!" Joanne declared eagerly. " They are on the porch, and Nancy and her mother are bringing them food. Let us go straight to the cabin, Mother, and hear them talk!" For Joanne thought it would be a great adventure to hear the Indian braves talk in their own language. " And, Mother dear, Indians always like presents. You could give them the basket of jelly, and I could give them the necklaces I made for Nancy and Lucy," and reaching into her deep pocket Joanne drew out the strings of shells that caught for an instant the rays of sunlight and shone and sparkled so that Mrs. Clarke exclaimed:

"Why, they are even prettier than beads!" much to Joanne's delight.

"If we walk straight along the path to the cabin they will see we are not afraid," said Mrs. Clarke, remembering that Indians always admired courage, and would often treat a captive who proved his brave spirit with kindness.

They now turned toward the Wagners' cabin, and Joanne talked eagerly of what Nancy and Lucy would say to see them coming straight across the clearing toward the Indians, for she was sure the red men would prove friendly. But Mrs. Clarke was not so confident, and held Joanne's hand closely, determined not to be separated from her little daughter.

As they stepped from the shelter of the woods into the clearing the Indians, who had been lounging on the steps of the cabin, sprang to their feet, their keen eyes fixed upon the woman and child who came so steadily on toward them.

As Joanne and her mother neared the house Joanne suddenly drew her hand from her mother's clasp and ran forward, and before Mrs. Clarke could overtake her Joanne was standing before one of the Indians holding out the basket of jellies in one hand while the necklaces of shells dangled from the other.

"Thayendangea! My mother brings you a gift of jelly, made of wild plums, and I have made necklaces for your braves!" she said in a clear voice, looking up into the face of the tall Indian whose skin was not so deep a brown as those of his companions, and whose dress at once proclaimed him as a great chief. His moccasins were elegantly trimmed with beads, and he wore a short green coat with epaulets of silver, and by his side hung a fine silver-mounted cutlass. It was indeed the much dreaded Joseph Brant himself, whose Indian name "Thayendangea" Joanne had so often heard.

"Gifts indeed!" responded the chief, taking the basket and passing it on with a guttural word to the Indian who stood just behind him; but the necklaces he examined more carefully, and a little smile crept over his grim face.

"These are but necklaces for dolls; give them to your playmates," he said, but there was a trace of kindness in his voice, and Joanne exclaimed with evident satisfaction:

"Then I may really give them to Nancy and

Lucy," and she smiled up at the grim Indian warrior as if he were indeed a friend.

Mrs. Clarke stood with Mrs. Wagner in the open doorway, and Nancy and Lucy were watching Joanne with wondering eyes, while the Indians with grunts of satisfaction were devouring the jelly that had been meant for Mrs. Wagner.

Brant looked down at the little girl standing so fearlessly before him and his smile broadened as he asked:

" How did you know my name? "

" Because of your fine garments," Joanne promptly replied, and at this Brant chuckled with evident satisfaction.

" And are you not afraid of the great chief of the Mohawks? "

Joanne shook her head.

" I never did you any harm. I wouldn't hurt you," she declared soberly, and at her reply Brant laughed aloud, and turning toward the other Indians repeated in guttural exclamations what Joanne had said, at the same time pointing at Joanne, who was listening eagerly.

The three Indian warriors muttered approval, and now Brant took Joanne's hand and turned toward the silent group in the doorway. Fixing his glance on Mrs. Clarke he said:

"This little maid is braver than most white men. What is her father's name?"

"John Clarke," said Joanne's mother.

"And is he loyal to King George of England?" questioned Brant.

"He believes in justice, Brant," Mrs. Clarke responded.

"Your daughter comes well by her courage, Madam," replied Brant, "and I mean to be her friend. Here," and he drew a ring of carefully wrought silver from his little finger and slipped it on Joanne's thumb. "Wear this, little maid, and forget not to be brave! Courage is your best protection; but with this ring no Mohawk will ever do you harm!"

Still holding Joanne by the hand he swung her about to face the three Indians, and speaking in the Mohawk tongue, bade them look well and make sure that they would remember that the little white maid was henceforth to be protected by every Mohawk. He bade Joanne hold up the hand on which he had placed his silver ring, and the Indians nodded silently.

"We will meet again!" he said briefly, with

a nod toward the group in the doorway; and, closely followed by his braves, he strode across the clearing and vanished into the forest.

" 'Tis almost more than I can believe!" declared Mrs. Wagner, looking at Joanne as if expecting the little girl would suddenly disappear.

And now Nancy and Lucy ran toward her; Mrs. Clarke and Mrs. Wagner began to talk earnestly over what Brant had said, while Nancy looked admiringly at Joanne's silver ring, and declared that her friend was as brave as Brant himself.

" He told Mother that he only wanted food for his braves," Nancy explained. " And they have taken away all our pork, and our store of corn. I know not what Father will say when he comes in from planting."

" He will be only glad we are safe," declared Lucy, who was admiring her shell necklace, and now added: " I think the Indian chief will remember these necklaces, don't you, Joanne? And may it not be that Nancy and I will be the safer for wearing them?"

Nancy and Joanne agreed hopefully that this might be true, and the two Wagner girls decided they would never leave home without wearing the shell necklaces.

Joanne was sure that she had never had so pleasant a visit. Mrs. Wagner spoke more than once of her young visitor's courage, and Nancy and Lucy could talk of but little else; and it was not until Joanne and her mother were again in the canoe that the little girl realized that her mother had been unusually thoughtful and silent.

CHAPTER III

A FAIRY'S VISIT

THE May afternoon was nearing twilight as Joanne and her mother paddled down the river. Joanne had taken off her sunbonnet, which she wore as little as possible, and, as she looked across the peaceful river and saw the blossom-bordered shores where the wild cherry trees overhung the stream and here and there crept up the green hillsides, Joanne smiled happily, quite sure that the Mohawk Valley was the most beautiful place in all the world.

It had been a wonderful day, she thought, glancing at the silver ring and recalling the promise of the Mohawk chief, and then Joanne again wondered why her mother had said so little of Brant's gift. Could it be that her mother did not want the chief's friendship?

But Joanne did not speak of this until they had reached their own cove and had drawn the canoe well up on the shore; then slipping her hand into her mother's she said soberly:

28

" Mother, are you not glad that the Indian chief is our friend? "

Mrs. Clarke looked down at her little daughter in surprise.

" Why, Joanne! Of course I am. Had it not been for your fearlessness that so pleased him we might even now be his captives," she answered, tightening her clasp on the little girl's hand.

Joanne's face brightened, and she gave a little skip as she so often did when well pleased.

" Then I could journey to Albany in safety, could I not, Mother dear? You know how often Grandma Clarke has sent us word that as soon as it was safe for a little maid to journey she would like well for me to come for a long visit. And would it not be a fine sight to see a real church, and houses made of bricks, such as you tell me may be seen in Albany, and shops with all manner of fine toys! Oh, Mother! how soon do you think someone traveling to Albany will take me? " and Joanne looked up at her mother, as if confident that Mrs. Clarke would agree that it might now be possible for her little daughter to make the long-hoped-for visit to the fine town of Albany. But Mrs. Clarke shook her head.

" Talk not of visits, Joanne," she said gravely.

" Your father's errand to Schenectady was to enlist in General Schuyler's army. If he reaches home to-night it will be but to bid us farewell until such time as the American cause triumphs; and you and I, Joanne, must do our best with the garden and to keep our home safe until his return."

Joanne's fingers clasped more closely about her mother's, and her smile vanished.

" Must Father go? " she asked.

" Indeed he must, Joanne; and you and I must do our part to win America's freedom by being brave and taking good care of our home. And it will be good news for your father to hear that your courage has won Brant's friendship," and Mrs. Clarke's voice was so cheerful that Joanne looked up hopefully, and she resolved to do her best to take her father's place: to work in the garden, care for the young chickens, and perhaps even protect her mother from danger; and she suddenly recalled the words of the Mohawk chief: " Courage is your best protection," and with a glance at her silver ring, Joanne had no fear of danger.

Mr. Clarke did not return that night, and it was nearly a week later when they received his message: he had been sent with other newly enlisted American soldiers to protect Fort Stanwix, the Fort Schuyler of earlier days and that was again renamed Fort Schuyler, and knew not when he might return home.

But the spring days were busy ones at the cabin home. Mrs. Clarke and Joanne planted their garden, that would provide them with food later on, cared for the brown cow, that Joanne was learning to milk, and looked after the big flock of chickens. Indoors Mrs. Clarke was busy at her spinning-wheel that they might have a good stock of yarn for knitting stockings for the coming winter, and Joanne, like every little American girl of Revolutionary days, could knit as well and rapidly as her mother. She could " take up " the stitches for a stocking; knit " seam " or " plain," " set the heel," and " toe-off," and when Nancy and Lucy came to visit her in the early spring they had brought their knitting-work as did their mother; and now, in late May, Joanne each day did her " stent," as it was called, knitting a certain number of rows on a stocking.

But the May sun was up at an early hour, and the days were long enough for Joanne to help

with the garden, knit her " stent," and have time
to run down to her playhouse on the bluff above
the river. Sometimes she would take her knitting-work, and sitting at the entrance of the cave,
her family of corn-cob dolls beside her, she would
look up the river toward distant Fort Schuyler
and think about her father and wish that she
might see him.

Joanne had to play alone most of the time,
for their nearest neighbors, the Eatons, who lived
just beyond the bluffs, were all grown-up people,
and Nancy and Lucy were too far away to come
as often as Joanne would like to have them; so
the little girl had " made up " various games that
she could play by herself.

The corn-cob dolls were a great help in these
games. Sometimes they would be English soldiers, captured by Americans and imprisoned in
the cave until pardoned by Joanne, who, she
would announce, was General Philip Schuyler,
and that she would pardon the prisoners if they
would no longer fight against America.

One warm afternoon, some days after Joanne's
visit to Nancy and Lucy, she climbed the rough
path to her playhouse, and sat down just outside the entrance. It had been an unusually

warm day, and all the morning Joanne had been at work in the garden; she had helped wash dishes, and then her mother had said: " No more work for you to-day, my dear. You may go where you please and do what you like until sunset," and Joanne had at once run down to the river, drawn off her moccasins and paddled happily about the sandy cove. Then she had built a fine fort of sand and pebbles close at the water's edge, and at last had climbed the bluff to the tiny cave.

" I do wish Nancy and Lucy were here to play games," she thought, looking at the row of corncob dolls set against a flat stone at the rear of the cave, and wishing that like dolls in a fairy story that her mother had once told her, they would suddenly walk and talk; and Joanne began to wonder if there really were tiny creatures called fairies who could do anything they pleased, and suddenly she heard a little tinkling voice say:

" Why, of course! Look at me! "

And there, standing on the toe of Joanne's moccasin, was the most wonderful and beautiful thing that Joanne could possibly imagine: a tiny creature no taller than one of Joanne's fingers, and wearing a dress of silvery green that seemed to float about it like mist. Joanne could hardly see its face, and now she dared hardly breathe for fear it would vanish. In one hand the fairy held a shining wand. As Joanne looked the little creature floated upward and there was a sound of tiny bells, a lovely fragrance as of honeysuckle blossoms, and then silence.

Joanne drew a long breath, and looked cautiously about. Just at her feet the tall grass waved in the springtime air; it was silvery-green like the fairy's dress, but the fairy had vanished.

Joanne stood up, peering into the cave. No fairy there. She looked out over the river, but no tiny floating creature was to be seen.

"It was a fairy!" she declared aloud. "It spoke to me!" And now more than ever Joanne wished that Nancy and Lucy had been with her that they, too, might have seen and heard the wonderful creature.

"I won't tell Mother," Joanne decided. "She would say I fell asleep and dreamed a fairy. But I am sure I was awake. Oh! I do wish it would come back," and for several days Joanne spent hours at her playhouse, wide awake and watching eagerly. But she never again saw the little creature in its misty green dress, holding a shining wand, but she henceforth believed in fairies; and, when she was really a grown-up woman, would declare that when she was a little girl she had seen one.

It was the day after the fairy's visit that Nancy and Lucy came to stay for two days at the Clarkes' cabin. Mrs. Wagner came with them, but stopped only for a brief rest on her way to visit her sister who lived two miles further on up the river.

"I will return in good season on Thursday," she said, and Joanne and her mother were both well pleased to have Nancy and Lucy for company.

The little girls at once began to make plans. First of all they were eager to see Joanne's playhouse, and as they started toward the bluff Nancy bade Joanne notice that both she and Lucy were wearing the shell necklaces that Joanne had made for them.

They had nearly reached the playhouse when Nancy grasped Joanne by the arm and whispered in a frightened tone: "Crouch down, Joanne!" and with her other hand drew Lucy down beside her as she kneeled in the tall grass.

"Indians!" she whispered to Joanne.

CHAPTER IV

NANCY AND LUCY

"Indians!" Joanne echoed, while the frightened Lucy began to whimper, and they all three crouched low in the grass; for the Indian allies of the British were the terror of every loyal American living in Mohawk Valley, and the three girls well knew that, even with Brant's silver ring as a protection, their surest safety was to escape notice.

Joanne's glance followed Nancy's and she saw a canoe coming down the river filled with Indian braves. It was near the shore, and for a time Joanne feared they meant to land at the cove at the foot of the bluff; but they paddled steadily up-stream, and Joanne crept through the grass to the edge of the bluff and watched the canoe until it was hidden by the trees overhanging the river.

"They are gone," she declared, as she returned to the two frightened little girls who still cowered in the grass. "They are paddling straight up-stream, so we need not fear!"

" Oh, Joanne! Do you know why my mother has gone to see Aunt Elizabeth? " questioned the still frightened Nancy. " She has gone to bid her pack her silver spoons and clothing and take her children and journey to Albany as soon as she can. It is that, Joanne, my mother was urging upon yours when she bade her good-bye. Do you not think your mother will consent to go with us when my mother returns? "

" To Albany! " exclaimed Joanne, for a moment wholly forgetting the Indians and thinking how wonderful it would be to go to Albany; to see where the Mohawk River entered the broad Hudson, and where ships from far-off countries brought cargoes of silks and spices, of china dishes, and even dolls with heads of china.

While Joanne's mind was filled with all these wonders Nancy talked on eagerly. She had jumped up from her hiding-place in the grass, and was telling Joanne of her father's plan to start down the river trail toward Albany. Mr. Wagner was lame, but Nancy said he meant to load their household goods on an ox-cart and to start as soon as possible.

" You could stay with your grandmother in her fine brick house," continued Nancy. " My father says it is near St. Peter's Church, where there are bells that ring on Sunday and on great occasions. Would you not well like to hear them, Joanne? And we shall sleep a night on the way, and stop to eat by some cool spring! Oh, Joanne! 'Twill be a fine journey. I do hope Aunt Elizabeth and little Floyd and Jane will come early on Thursday and that your mother will be all ready to start."

"But my mother said naught of meaning to go," said Joanne. "It may be she does not mean to, for only last week she said it was no time to travel."

"But she *must!*" declared Nancy. "The Eatons have already gone. My father says it is no longer safe in this part of the valley until the British General Burgoyne is driven away!"

"Oh!" said Joanne, a little smile creeping over her face. "That may happen any day. I do not think we need fear, for I heard my father say that General Schuyler means to capture him. But I'd well like to visit Albany."

"Let us run back to the house and ask your mother if she will be ready to start on Thursday," suggested Nancy, and Joanne promptly agreed, and calling to Lucy, who had wandered into the

playhouse and was amusing herself with the corn-
cob dolls, the two older girls started toward the
cabin talking eagerly of the possible adventures
and pleasures of the journey to Albany. As
they ran into the big living-room the whirr of
Mrs. Clarke's spinning-wheel made them stop
suddenly, and Joanne quickly realized that,
whatever her neighbors might do, her mother
meant to remain in her own home.

Mrs. Clarke smiled and nodded as she carefully twirled the smooth thread of wool, and
brought the big wheel to a standstill.

"You are going with us to Albany, are you
not, Mistress Clarke?" Nancy questioned eagerly. "You and Joanne will be all ready to
start with us, will you not?" and Nancy's blue
eyes looked confidently up at Joanne's mother.

"No," Mrs. Clarke responded quietly. "I
told your mother, Nancy, that it seems wiser and
safer to remain here. There are small bands of
Indians moving along the river, or through the
forests, and until the Americans have conquered
the British there will be no safety; but I think
it best for Joanne and me to stay here."

Nancy made no reply, but her smile vanished
and she looked at Joanne pleadingly as if expect-

ing her to persuade Mrs. Clarke to change her
decision; but Joanne was twisting the silver ring
on her thumb, and seemed to have nothing to say.

"Where is Lucy?" Mrs. Clarke asked.

"She's just outside, I guess," replied Nancy,
too disappointed by Mrs. Clarke's decision to
give much thought to her younger sister.

"Well, bid her come in. You must all be
ready for supper, and I have a little surprise for
you all!" and Mrs. Clarke turned toward the
kitchen, while Joanne and Nancy ran to the
porch to call Lucy.

But Lucy was not to be seen.

"Oh, dear! She stayed in the cave playing
with your dolls, Joanne," exclaimed Nancy.
"I'll have to go after her," and Nancy ran off
toward the shore, while Joanne followed her
mother toward the kitchen.

"What is the 'surprise,' Mother?" she asked,
as she stood in the open doorway.

"Run away until I call you, Joanne," said
Mrs. Clarke from the storeroom. "This is a
truly surprise! Go out on the porch with Nancy
and Lucy; I will call you in a jiffy!"

Joanne ran back to the porch. For the moment, in wondering what the "surprise" could

possibly be, she forgot all Nancy had said about journeying to Albany, and stood waiting to see Nancy and Lucy coming toward the cabin.

" Why doesn't Nancy hurry? " she thought a little impatiently, as the moments slipped by and there was no sight or sound of Nancy and Lucy.

" All ready! " called Mrs. Clarke from the kitchen, and Joanne called back:

" They haven't come yet, Mother."

" Run and call them," responded Mrs. Clarke, and Joanne sped off down the path. When she reached the foot of the bluff she called: " Nancy! Lucy! " but there was no response.

" Oh, dear! I s'pose they are in the cave and can't hear," she said aloud, and climbed softly to the opening to her playhouse.

" Supper and the ' surprise ' are all ready and waiting for you to come," she called, and then, wondering that everything seemed so quiet, she crouched down and looked into the little cave. There was no one there, nor was there any trace of Nancy or Lucy.

For a moment Joanne could not believe but that they were hiding from her; but after again calling their names, and searching the grassy hillside she became frightened and ran back to the cabin.

Mrs. Clarke was standing on the porch, and as she saw Joanne fleeing up the path she hastened to meet her.

"What is it, Joanne? Where are Nancy and Lucy?" she asked anxiously.

"Oh, Mother! I can't find them. I've looked everywhere. They are gone!"

CHAPTER V

Mrs. Clarke was sure that the little girls could not be far away.

"Perhaps they are hiding, Joanne, and when they hear me call they will come," she said as they hurried toward the river.

"There they are, Mother! There they are!" exclaimed Joanne, darting off as two small figures came hurrying toward them. Nancy began to tell what had befallen them before Joanne reached her, while Lucy sauntered on behind the anxious Nancy as if not much concerned by Mrs. Clarke's anxiety, for which she was wholly to blame.

"I ran away!" she now proudly announced. "And Nancy ran after me, and couldn't catch me!"

"That's just what she did!" said Nancy wrathfully, "and I shall tell Mother."

But Lucy did not seem much alarmed at this, and Mrs. Clarke was too relieved to have them both safe to blame Lucy for her mischief.

"I'm hungry!" said Lucy, a little plaintively,

43

and this instantly reminded Joanne of the promised surprise, and she turned toward her mother who smiled at her little daughter's questioning look, and said:

" Take Nancy and Lucy to your room, Joanne, where you can all make yourselves tidy, and I will call you in a few minutes."

Although Joanne's home was built of logs, and far away from any town or settlement, it was comfortable and well furnished: besides the big living-room and kitchen there were two chambers, and Joanne's room had two windows that overlooked the cleared land on the west of the cabin, and that stretched down to the river. There were curtains of striped linen at the windows, and the floor was covered with a bright carpet woven of rags. In one corner were a number of low shelves; one of these shelves held many bright-colored pebbles and queerly shaped rocks that Joanne had discovered and brought home, and a bird's nest made of hair and grass firmly woven together. On the upper shelves were the books that were Joanne's most treasured possessions. There was " Pilgrim's Progress," that Grandma Clarke had sent her on her tenth birthday, and a wonderful book of colored pictures that her own mother had made, with a verse for every picture. Mrs. Clarke had drawn and colored the pictures, and written a verse for each, and then bound the book in covers of soft deerskin. She had done this on winter evenings, by candlelight, with Joanne sitting beside her at the round table drawn up in front of the blazing fire, and some of the verses Joanne's father had laughingly suggested and her mother had written them down; so it was no wonder that Joanne thought "Joanne's Book," as her mother had named it, was the most delightful book that any little girl could possess.

Nancy and Lucy Wagner were usually eager to be allowed to look at it, to read some favorite verse aloud, and to exclaim over the picture of the two kittens who became King and Queen of Catland, as the verse beneath the picture declared:

"Here is Queen Pussie Grimalkin—
    The greatest of cats,
    To whom all cats in Catland
    Must take off their hats.
    And here is her brother
    King Thomas so bold,
    In a crown all of diamonds
    And a sword of pure gold!"

But now neither Nancy nor Lucy even glanced toward the corner shelves, for Lucy objected to having her tangled yellow curls brushed, and poor Nancy had begun to wish that her mother had taken Lucy with her or that they had all remained in their own home; and it was finally Joanne who persuaded Lucy to stop running about the room by saying:

"What do you suppose my mother's 'surprise' for us is?"

"'Surprise'?" echoed the little girl.

"Why, yes. She has a surprise for us all waiting in the kitchen as soon as we are ready," Joanne replied, and now Lucy urged Nancy to fix her hair as quickly as possible, and submitted to having her hands and face washed.

"I hope the s'prise is something good to eat!" declared Lucy, and would have rushed off to the kitchen to find out had not Nancy taken a firm hold of her gingham skirt.

"Lucy Mehitable Wagner! I'm 'most ashamed of you!" poor Nancy declared, almost ready to cry over her little sister's thoughtlessness. "Did not Mother tell us to be polite, and not to say a word about anything to eat, and not to make any trouble for Joanne's mother! And just see what ——"

But at that moment Mrs. Clarke called that supper was ready, and Nancy, still keeping a tight hold on the eager Lucy, followed Joanne to the kitchen.

The May twilight had now faded to dusk; Mrs. Clarke had lighted candles, and the white cover of the table, the shining pewter plates and mugs, together with the blue pitcher in the centre filled with the branch of late-blossoming white lilac, gave the room a festive appearance, and Nancy and Joanne exclaimed in admiration. The whole room seemed transformed. But Lucy, suddenly free of Nancy's restraining clasp, darted toward the table calling out:

" Gingerbread dolls! Oh, goody! goody!" and would have seized a most tempting figure made of gingerbread, whose eyes were of white sugar, and whose nose and mouth were bits of sugared walnuts, had not Nancy reached her in time to seize Lucy's outstretched hand. Poor Nancy felt that her small sister was bringing disgrace on all the Wagner family.

" Please, Mrs. Clarke, she knows better than to act so rudely. 'Tis not that our mother has not taught her to behave!" pleaded Nancy, looking up at Mrs. Clarke.

"I am sure Lucy knows the proper way for a young lady to take her seat at a table," Mrs. Clarke responded, with a smile for the troubled Nancy. "And now let us pretend that Lady Washington is expected to arrive at any moment and all be on our best behavior!"

"Yes! Yes!" exclaimed Joanne. "Let us have a 'pretend' dinner party. It's fun, Nancy!" she declared, turning to her friend. "Mother and I have a lot of 'pretends,' don't we, Mother?"

"We do, indeed," Mrs. Clarke agreed.

"I am going to be Lady Washington!" Lucy announced firmly, and before Nancy could object Mrs. Clarke said that would be a good plan, for it was well known that Mrs. George Washington was always kind and thoughtful toward others, and most elegant in her manners.

"You and Nancy, Joanne, must make your best curtseys to Lady Washington," said Mrs. Clarke gravely, as she seated the smiling Lucy at the head of the table; and the candle-lit kitchen made a pretty picture indeed as Nancy and Joanne curtseyed low before the small figure seated at the head of the table who in her turn bowed low and said that she was " well pleased to meet such polite ladies of Mohawk Valley."

For a few moments the little girls were so taken up with their play that they forgot Mrs. Clarke's fine gingerbread dolls, one for each of them, that stood beside their plates. But after Joanne and Nancy had taken their places at the table and " Lady Washington " had politely urged them to help themselves, they both declared the " dolls " were the finest surprise possible; and even Lucy restrained her desire to bite off a hand or foot of her gingerbread surprise until supper was over and " Lady Washington " disappeared and she was again little Lucy Wagner.

But it seemed as if something of Lady Washington's good manners remained with Lucy, for she was so polite in her replies to whoever spoke to her, and later on so ready to go to bed that Nancy began to fear that her little sister might be ill. But Lucy had decided that henceforth she was going to pretend always that she was Lady Washington, and with that resolve she went happily to sleep.

CHAPTER VI

" PRETEND " GAMES

NANCY and Lucy were both eager to hear
more about the " pretend " games that Joanne
and her mother so enjoyed, and Joanne promised that she would tell them the next morning.

" We will have all day to-morrow; your
mother will not be here until Thursday," she
reminded them.

" But you will have your lesson hour, and to
work in the garden, and I know not what you
have to do indoors," said Nancy.

" To-morrow I am to do exactly as I please
all day," Joanne declared, with her usual little
dancing skip to express her delight, " and I have
already thought of the grandest ' pretend
game.' " But although Nancy urged her to tell
what it was Joanne would only shake her head
and say that they must wait until morning; so
the little girls finally gave up teasing her and
went to bed, their thoughts full of the pleasures
of the coming day.

The little household were up at an early hour,

and before Nancy and Lucy responded to Joanne's call to breakfast Nancy had warned her small sister that she was expected to behave better than on the previous day.

" I know not what Mrs. Clarke thinks of your naughtiness," Nancy solemnly declared, " but promise, Lucy, to do your best to behave well; try and behave just as I do."

Lucy readily promised; she was usually good-natured, and was now quite ready to do whatever Nancy suggested, and she followed her sister to the kitchen endeavoring to walk exactly as Nancy did, and said " Good-morning, Mistress Clarke," in a voice so much like Nancy's that Joanne, who had been watching Lucy's effort to move in exactly the same way as did Nancy, smiled at the little girl's cleverness.

At the table Lucy was very quiet, eating her milk and porridge and only speaking when someone asked her a question; but Joanne noticed that Lucy held her pewter spoon just as Nancy did, and that when Nancy stopped eating her little sister did the same, and at last Joanne exclaimed:

" Lucy does everything you do, Nancy, and in just the same way! "

" I wish she always would," Nancy responded

primly, with an anxious glance toward her little sister.

" I am going to!" Lucy announced, nodding her head so solemnly that Joanne laughed aloud, and Nancy's grave face softened, and she thought that Lucy, with her yellow curls and blue eyes, was just the right kind of a little sister, in spite of her mischievous ways.

" Now tell us about ' pretends,' " said Nancy, as they finished their breakfast and she began helping Joanne clear the table; for even a day of playtime, such as Joanne was to have with her little visitors, did not mean that Joanne would not fulfill the simple household duties that were in those days taught to every little girl.

" Now tell us about ' pretends,' " echoed Lucy, who close at her sister's heels was carrying her porridge-bowl to the table near the kitchen door where stood a big pan of hot water in which Joanne would wash the dishes.

" Just as soon as we get outdoors," whispered Joanne, and Nancy at once agreed, and in a short time the three little girls slipped out of the open kitchen door and wandered to the shade of a big butternut tree, Joanne talking as fast as possible of the game she had planned.

" You see, Nancy, ' pretend ' is just make-believe, and let's make believe to be an army! "

" ' An army '? " questioned the amazed Nancy, while Lucy, in exactly Nancy's voice of surprise, echoed, " ' An army '! "

" Yes, I'll tell you how! Come on! " said Joanne leading the way across the rough field toward the edge of the forest.

Nancy and Lucy were close behind her and Joanne kept on with the story of her plan. They could, she declared, make " make-believe " soldiers out of sticks and branches. " I'll be General Philip Schuyler and you can be General Nicholas Herkimer, Nancy, and Lucy can be ——" and Joanne waited a moment thoughtfully trying to think who Lucy should represent.

" I'll be General Herkimer, too. I'm going to be whatever Nancy is! " Lucy declared, and in spite of all Joanne could say, and of Nancy's effort to convince her small sister that two people could not be one person, Lucy would only repeat: " I'm going to be whatever Nancy is."

" Well, never mind! Let's begin," said Joanne, and the three little girls pulled and tugged the broken branches of the forest trees out into the clearing, and under Joanne's direction began to make their " army."

They stuck the taller branches into the earth, and, with vines and tough grasses, tied on other branches as arms. They managed to make from leaves and brakes queer looking hats that were not unlike the three-cornered hats worn by the soldiers of the American Army, and at last a dozen figures were completed, standing two by two not far from the edge of the woodland.

Each one of these make-believe " soldiers " bore the name of some brave officer of the American Army: for both Joanne and Nancy daily heard their parents, as well as any visitor who might chance to enter their home, speak of the men who were doing their best to defend the liberties of America.

General Washington, Lafayette, the young Frenchman who was giving his service to the patriots, Major Benedict Arnold; and in their own Mohawk Valley the names of St. Clair, Gansevoort, Schuyler, Herkimer, Dayton and Willett were known to every settler as the leaders of the soldiers who were determined to support America. So now Joanne gave each of the queer figures a name that stood for loyalty and courage. Nancy repeated each one, and whatever Nancy said Lucy would at once say after her, at the same time endeavoring to move and speak exactly like Nancy, much to Joanne's amusement, although Nancy was soon vexed and impatient; but whenever she would ask Lucy to stop Lucy would say:

"You told me to behave just as you do, and I'm going to. Whatever you do I'm going to do," and Lucy instantly assumed the same troubled expression that Nancy's face now wore.

"Now, 'General Herkimer,' you and I must drill our soldiers!" said Joanne; and Nancy, echoed by her small sister, promptly responded:

"All ready, General Schuyler," and for a time the little girls amused themselves with their "army." It was Joanne who at last suggested that it must be time for dinner, and they turned toward the cabin.

"Let's have one game of 'hide and seek,'" said Nancy. "Your mother is sure to call us when dinner is ready, is she not, Joanne?"

Joanne agreed, and pointing her finger toward Nancy, then at Lucy and herself began the "Counting out" verse that her Grandmother Clarke had taught her:

" ' Intry, Mintry, Cutry, Corn,
Apple seed and Apple thorn.
Wire, Briar, Limber, Lock,
Three geese in a flock.
One flew east and one flew west
And one flew over the black crow's nest.' "

" You're It, Joanne! You're It! " declared Nancy; and Joanne turned her back to Nancy and Lucy, shut her eyes, and began to count the hundred, while Nancy, with Lucy close at her heels, sped off to hide.

" Go away, Lucy, and hide by yourself," commanded Nancy angrily. " You can't hide with me! I won't have you. You act silly! I'm just as 'shamed of you as I can be! " and Nancy stamped her foot, and looked at Lucy so angrily that for a moment the little girl did not know what to say; then the angry tears filled her eyes and she exclaimed: " I'll hide where you'll never find me, Nancy Wagner, see if I don't! "

" I wish you would," said Nancy in a whisper, and the sisters each fled in opposite directions.

Joanne's clear: " One hundred! 'Look east, look west, the crow is coming to find your nest,' " warned Nancy, who was crouching among the " army," that she must not move. But Lucy did not hear the call.

CHAPTER VII

CAPTIVES

"JOANNE! Joanne!"

Mrs. Clarke stepped out of the kitchen and walked a little way toward the clearing calling the girls to the midday meal, and, as she looked toward the woodland, she stopped suddenly with a whispered exclamation:

"Soldiers!" she said, and then looking more closely began to wonder what the queer figures really were, and when Joanne and Nancy came running to meet her Mrs. Clarke pointed toward the "Army" and asked gravely:

"What are those strange things at the edge of the woods? At first I really thought they were soldiers!"

"Oh! Did you truly, Mother?" exclaimed the delighted Joanne. "Well, they are. The first two are General Ethan Allen and General Nathaniel Herkimer——"

But Nancy interrupted by darting suddenly back across the clearing, leaving Mrs. Clarke and Joanne to gaze after her wonderingly.

57

" She has gone after Lucy," Joanne said; and then as she and her mother turned back toward the cabin, Joanne went on telling the list of names that she had bestowed on the " Army."

Mrs. Clarke listened smilingly, and praised Joanne. " At a little distance your soldiers made of sticks and leaves might easily be mistaken for real men," she said, without the slightest idea that these queer figures were really to be so mistaken, and thus protect the cabin.

" And may I leave the ' Army ' just as it is, Mother? " asked Joanne.

Mrs. Clarke promptly agreed. " I hope the ' Army ' will not fall apart until your father has seen them," she said, and Joanne declared that she meant to visit them each day and keep them in repair.

" Dinner is waiting, and will be none the better for our delay. Call Nancy and Lucy," said Mrs. Clarke, turning toward the cabin.

Joanne could see Nancy running along the border of the forest searching for Lucy, and ran to join her. From time to time Nancy or Joanne would call: " The game is finished, Lucy. Dinner's ready. Don't hide any longer! "

But there was no response, and Nancy now

suddenly recalled Lucy's declaration that she would hide where Nancy could never find her.

" You don't suppose Lucy has run off into the forest and can't find her way back? " she asked, and for a moment Joanne was silent for she had begun to fear this very thing; and Joanne well knew all the dangers that might easily happen to a little girl who wandered from the trails into the stretch of unbroken woodland.

" We'll find her, Nancy," Joanne declared. " Even if she has hidden in the woods she can't be far away, and I know all the paths. Come on, Nancy," and Joanne ran forward along a narrow pathway that led between tall chestnuts and towering pines and finally ended in a thick growth of brakes nearly as tall as Joanne. But they made their way through these, across a tiny open space, and every few moments they would stop and call: " Lucy! Lucy! " and sometimes search behind the thickly growing underbrush where the noise of some chittering squirrel scampering away had made them believe for a moment that Lucy was close at hand.

Nancy began to feel that Lucy must have returned to the cabin. " She would surely answer if she heard us call," she said, " and very likely

she and your mother are now eating dinner while
we are searching for her. I do not know why
Lucy behaves so badly," concluded Nancy, who
was now tired and hungry and for the moment
forgot her fear that her little sister might indeed
have hidden herself where Nancy might not find
her.

"Listen!" whispered Joanne, bending forward
to peer through an opening in the woodland.
"I can see something move, Nancy," she added
quickly. "I do believe it is Lucy hiding behind
those tall trees."

"Call her!" urged Nancy; "and I mean that
Mother and Father shall know all her naughtiness. I——"

But Joanne's "Ssshh——" made her stop
suddenly. "Let's creep up close to her before
we call," whispered Joanne, "or she may run
and hide again."

Nancy nodded her agreement, and the two
girls now made their way cautiously in the direction where a figure crouching against a tree had
made Joanne confident that they had discovered
Lucy; but it seemed a longer distance than they
had thought.

"I do believe she saw us and keeps hiding.

I'm going to call her," Nancy declared, and before Joanne could warn her to be silent Nancy's loud " Lucy! Lucy Wagner!" echoed through the forest and at that very instant an Indian appeared from behind a tree and seizing Nancy with one hand and Joanne with the other he drew them rapidly along with him.

Nancy began to cry, but a remembrance of Brant's words: " Courage is your best protection " flashed across Joanne's thoughts, and she made no sound as she struggled to keep pace with the long strides of her captor.

"Lucy! Lucy!" moaned Nancy, until Joanne said: " Maybe he's taking us to Lucy," and at this Nancy's cries and moans came to an end. She knew Lucy must be found, and she gained a little courage from Joanne's sturdy silence.

The Indian now looked at Joanne with an approving nod, and muttered some words that neither of the girls could understand, but he kept on at the same rapid pace. Joanne soon realized that they were now too deep in the forest to find their own way back to the cabin; she began to be sure that, wherever Lucy might be, this Indian knew nothing about her and that he was taking Nancy and herself to some far-off Indian encampment.

"Your ring, Joanne, your ring," wailed the frightened and unhappy Nancy, as the Indian came to a standstill near the bank of a swiftly flowing stream that danced over a bed of clear sand and vanished into the shadowy woodland.

Instantly Joanne held up her hand with Brant's silver ring encircling her thumb, and looking up into the painted face of the Indian warrior she said: "Brant's ring! To keep me safe!"

At the name "Brant," the Indian's eyes widened. "Know Brant?" he questioned.

"Oh, Joanne! Tell him Brant is your friend," wailed Nancy, who had sunk to the ground the moment the Indian had released his grasp. The brave now gave her a scowling glance, and then turned to question Joanne.

"Know Brant?" he again asked.

"Yes. He gave me this ring. He said no Mohawk would harm me if he saw it," Joanne replied, doing her best to speak clearly and not to show fear.

Apparently the Indian understood. For a moment he stood silent, then he motioned to

Joanne to sit down beside Nancy and she obeyed.

"Oh, Joanne, where do you suppose he means to take us?" whimpered Nancy. "I don't believe that old ring is any good or he would say something about taking us home."

Joanne made no reply. She realized they were in danger. More than one white child in the Mohawk Valley had been taken captive and never returned to their family. Unless Brant's ring could protect them this might now be their fate. There was a choking feeling in Joanne's throat, and it was difficult to keep back her tears as her thoughts fled to her mother who, Joanne well knew, was even now anxious and unhappy over her disappearance, and Joanne resolved to do her best to make this Indian understand that the silver ring was indeed a protection, and she jumped up and again holding up her hand pointed to the silver ring and exclaimed: "Brant!"

The Indian now nodded. But the little girls realized he did not mean to go any farther, and they were tired enough to be glad to rest. It was evident he did not know much English, or, if he did, that he did not mean to say anything. He had thrown himself down near the stream and was apparently deciding what to do with his captives.

The woodland shadows began to deepen. Nancy and Joanne huddled close together, their eyes fixed on that motionless figure near the edge of the brook. Suddenly Joanne's clasp on Nancy's hand tightened. " He's gone, Nancy!" she whispered.

For a few moments neither of the little girls spoke; they peered fearfully about them. They did not dare move lest a savage voice might threaten them; but as the minutes passed and there was no sign of their captor's return Joanne gained courage and rose to her feet.

" He's run off and left us," she said in a low voice, and turned toward the brook, moving cautiously as if fearful that the slightest sound might bring the Indian back. She had reached the place where the brave had thrown himself when the glitter of beads caught her eye, and half-hidden in feathery moss she saw a flat skin purse and picked it up.

" What is it, Joanne? " whispered Nancy, who was close at her elbow.

" It's the Indian's pouch. See how flat it is!

There's nothing in it save a thin paper," replied Joanne, holding out the pouch of tanned deer-skin for Nancy to examine.

" The beads are pretty!" said Nancy, pointing to a figure of a bird worked on the pouch in red beads. " Put it in your pocket, Joanne; if he comes back he will be well pleased that you found it," said Nancy, and Joanne slipped the beaded case into the stout pocket of her skirt, and then kneeled down by the brook and drank thirstily, and Nancy quickly followed suit.

" I'm so hungry, Joanne; don't you s'pose we can find something to eat?" asked Nancy, as the two little girls arose from the edge of the stream and stood looking about the little clearing beneath the tall forest trees.

Joanne shook her head. " Too early for berries," she replied, " and it's getting toward sunset. Nancy, we'll have to stay here all night."

CHAPTER VIII

A NIGHT IN THE FOREST

For a brief moment the two little girls stood silent, each regarding the other as if expecting her companion to find a way out of their difficulties. It was Nancy who spoke first.

"Joanne! We mustn't stay here; not another minute," and she clasped Joanne's arm and began to draw her toward the stream. "The Indian may come back, and if he does he will surely not leave us again."

Joanne agreed, and, still speaking in whispers, they decided to follow the stream. Both Nancy and Joanne knew that the many brooks that tumbled down the wooded hillsides of Mohawk Valley all found their way to the river, and as they crawled over fallen trees, pushed their way through underbrush and now and then crossed little open spaces where wild flowers blossomed, or where beds of deep moss lay beneath wide-spreading trees, they encouraged each other by saying that very soon they would reach the Mohawk River and then it would be easy to find their way home.

66

But darkness was creeping through the woodland; they were tired and hungry, and as they stopped in a little circle of young spruce trees Joanne threw herself on the moss with a tired sigh, and said: "We can't go another step, Nancy!"

Nancy sank down beside her friend. "What can we do, Joanne?" she asked, her voice trembling with fear. "There are bears and wildcats in the forests, and what could we do if they came after us?"

"I don't know," murmured Joanne. "I'm almost too tired and hungry to think of anything, or to be afraid of anything. Do you know, Nancy, Mother had the nicest dinner all ready for us; there was chicken-pie, and hot corn bread and apple tarts."

Nancy moaned aloud. "'Apple tarts'!" she repeated, as if the loss of those dainties was the chief misfortune that had befallen them.

Crouched close together the two little girls whispered of plans for the morning: perhaps they would find the cabin of some settler near at hand; or might it not be they could really reach home! But as the long shadows deepened and darkness settled over the woodland the tired girls drifted into slumber and did not waken until the sun sent long beams of light into their hiding-place.

Joanne was the first to open her eyes, and she slipped away from Nancy for a drink from the cool stream, then she bathed her face and hands and endeavored to rebraid her hair. As she thus busied herself Joanne wondered if Lucy was safe at the cabin. " Maybe she hid under the porch, or behind the shed," she thought, " and is eating breakfast with my mother!" and Joanne sighed unhappily.

She had just started back toward the sleeping Nancy when she heard a queer sound further down the stream, and instantly remembered how often wandering bears, wolves and lynx were found near the brooks where they came to drink. But an instant later a clear whistle convinced the listening girl that the noise was made by some trapper or hunter near at hand, and Joanne now did her best to echo the musical notes. Twice she repeated the whistle she had heard, and stood listening; but a silence seemed to have settled upon the forest.

" Oh, dear!" she said aloud. " The man could not have heard my whistle! What can I do?" and she peered anxiously in the direction from which the sounds had come, and as she gazed a tall figure appeared almost in front of her. A man, dressed in a deerskin tunic and trousers, with moccasins on his feet, and wearing a three-cornered hat. His belt held a sheathed hunting knife, and he carried a rifle.

As Joanne looked at him she realized the stranger was as surprised as she was.

"By my faith! 'Tis a little maid!" he exclaimed, and Joanne began quickly to tell her story—for she well knew that any white man in the Mohawk Valley would protect a lost child.

Before she had finished her story Nancy came running to join them. "And we didn't have any dinner or supper!" she exclaimed.

"What about broiled trout?" said the man smilingly. "Sit you down here, and we'll soon have a bit to eat. Remember: you are not to take one step!" and he looked at them anxiously.

"We won't!" Nancy promised eagerly, and Joanne smiled, sure now that they need no longer go hungry or fear the wild beasts of the forest or capture by Indians. She had noticed that the man's eyes were as blue as Nancy's, and that his smile was as friendly as if he had always known them.

He was back before the little girls had time to wonder who their rescuer might be; and this time he brought with him a small knapsack, and a string of trout, which, he smilingly told them, he caught before sunrise.

"I was out to catch 'Red-bird,'" he added, "but from what you tell me, he's well on his way to meet General Burgoyne. I'd like well to have captured the fellow," he added, as if talking to himself, at the same time starting a brisk fire over which the trout were quickly broiled.

As the hungry girls feasted on these the man drew a package from his knapsack, opened it, and Joanne and Nancy could hardly refrain from clutching at the squares of corn bread that it held.

"Help yourselves, little maids," said the man, seating himself beside them and beginning his own breakfast.

"I never had so good a breakfast!" Nancy declared, and Joanne remembered to tell him that they were both greatly obliged to him. "And will you please take us home now?" she added, confident that this kindly man with the pleasant blue eyes would promptly agree.

"I'm bound for Albany. My canoe is at the mouth of this very stream. Where is your home?" he asked, and as Joanne and Nancy eagerly explained where the Clarke cabin stood the man shook his head gravely.

"The Indian surely brought you at a great pace. You are ten miles from home, nor can I spare the time to take you back. I must be in Albany, even though I have not secured the message. Nor can I leave two little maids in this wilderness," he concluded with his friendly smile.

"Joanne's grandmother lives in Albany," said Nancy thoughtfully; and then, remembering Lucy, she began to cry.

"But 'tis to-morrow, Nancy, that your own mother and father, your Aunt Elizabeth and all your family start for Albany," Joanne reminded her. "You will be there in time to welcome them; but I," and she turned toward the man, "I must go home. My father is at Fort Stanwix, and my mother is alone. She cannot spare me!"

The man shook his head gravely. "'Tis not possible, little maid. I am a scout in the service of the American Army. Even now General Burgoyne with his English army, his Canadians and Indians, is ready to march toward Albany. Such news as I have for General Schuyler cannot be delayed. Your grandmother at Albany will care for you, and send your mother word of your safety," and as he spoke he rose to his feet, shouldered his knapsack, and bade the little girls keep close beside him as he made his way toward the mouth of the stream.

Joanne tried her best to keep back her tears. She forgot that for many weeks she had hoped she might visit Albany. Her only wish now was to be safely at home with her mother.

But Nancy was now in good spirits; she felt sure that Lucy was safe with Mrs. Clarke, and was confident that the American scout would paddle Joanne and herself safely to Albany where her family would be sure to find her. But neither of the little girls spoke as they followed the man down the stream to the place where his canoe was hidden.

The sun was now well up, and the June day grew warm as the canoe moved swiftly down the stream. The two little girls, seated in the bottom of the canoe, whispered together of all that had befallen them.

"Was that a bird marked out in red beads on the Indian's pouch?" questioned Nancy.

"Yes! See how the beads shine." replied

Joanne, drawing the deerskin wallet from the deep pocket of her torn skirt and holding it toward Nancy.

The name " red-bird " had caught the attention of the scout and he turned a questioning glance over his shoulder.

" What's that? " he asked.

" It's a wallet the Indian dropped. There's a paper in it," replied Joanne.

CHAPTER IX

JOANNE MAKES A PROMISE

THE scout stared at Joanne and Nancy wonderingly, and held his paddle poised in air as if too surprised to speak; but after a few seconds he said:

"Do you mean to say *that* is Red-bird's wallet?" and he pointed toward the beaded pouch in Joanne's hand.

"I found it after the Indian ran off," Joanne explained, "and there is nothing in it but a thin paper."

The man reached out his hand and Joanne gave him the pouch; for a time the canoe drifted on as the scout opened the deerskin wallet and drew out the folded paper that he at once opened and read eagerly, his face startled and serious.

"'Tis as I thought!" he said, as if speaking to himself. "The British and their Indians mean to move toward Albany." Then with a smile he returned the paper to its wallet and held it toward Joanne.

74

" General Schuyler will be warned in good time. Here, the safest place for this, after all, will be in your pocket, little maid; but I trust your pocket is a strong one," and he glanced a little anxiously at Joanne's torn skirt.

" It is, indeed. 'Tis of stout gingham," Joanne answered.

" That is well. Listen now, carefully, and remember each word I say. That paper is a message from the Indian chief Brant, to the British General Burgoyne who is even now invading New York with his troops, Canadians and Indians. It is a message that must be in General Schuyler's hands as soon as may be. If aught befall me before we reach Albany you, little maids, must not fail to make sure that General Philip Schuyler, or some trusted and loyal American officer, receives Red-bird's pouch. Promise me!" and the friendly face of the scout was so grave, his blue eyes so serious as they met the glance of Joanne that both she and Nancy for the moment forgot all their own troubles and both responded:

" We promise," but Joanne added quickly:

" But what harm could befall you? "

A smile crept over the scout's face, and he answered lightly:

"What harm indeed; with two brave Americans to aid me I will surely reach Albany in safety. But, remember," and his tone grew serious, "it may well be that you two little maids are to do a great service to the great cause of America's freedom."

For a little time Nancy and Joanne whispered together, and the scout wielded his paddle as if determined to make up for lost time. The canoe darted past small wooded islands, past occasional small settlements near the river's edge, and then near high bluffs that cast long shadows across the stream, and both Nancy and Joanne had begun to be hungry and thirsty when the scout, at well past noonday, turned the prow of the canoe toward shore and they landed in a little cove so much like the cove near Joanne's home that she looked about half expecting to see the familiar cabin and cleared fields; but only thickly growing woods and a stretch of swampy ground could be seen; and Joanne looked longingly up the stream toward where her own home lay, but a word from the scout reminded her that there was no time to be wasted.

"You girls gather dry sticks for a fire," he said, "but go not out of sight of the canoe," and he was off.

"Do you think he has food in that bag?" Nancy asked, pointing to a leather bag stowed in one end of the canoe.

"It may be. Oh, Nancy, I like not to be going so far from home! 'Tis a good hundred miles to Albany, and 'twill be days before my mother can hear I am safe!" said Joanne, for the moment quite forgetting her resolve to be brave whatever happened.

But Nancy, sure that her own family might even now be on their way to Albany and that in another day she might be there waiting for their arrival, was only eager to hurry on, and answered smilingly:

"But, Joanne, just think! You can go straight to your Grandmother Clarke's fine house; and I must go with you, Joanne, for I have no place else to go, and you will have great news for your grandmother. You can tell her that your father is at Fort Stanwix, or Fort Schuyler, as many call it, and ——" but the return of the scout interrupted Nancy, and as he bade them bring the bag from the canoe, while he started a fire to cook the two plump partridges he had so cleverly snared, the girls for the time forgot everything else in the preparation of the midday meal.

"Open the bag," said the man, with his friendly smile, and Joanne and Nancy began to untie the stout thongs of deerskin that fastened it and in a few moments Joanne exclaimed:

"Potatoes!" and smiled at Nancy as if she had discovered some rare fruit.

Beside potatoes the bag held coffee and a package of sugar, as well as bacon and salt. The scout baked the potatoes in the hot ashes, broiled the partridge, and made coffee in a battered old tin that was also in the bag; and while these were cooking Joanne and Nancy pulled the bark from an old birch log near at hand and made a number of dishes from the stout silvery bark.

If breakfast had been welcome to the hungry girls this noonday meal by the river tasted even better: the broiled partridge, the well-baked potatoes, and the hot, sweetened coffee seemed a feast indeed; and when they helped the scout to gather up the food and then took their places in the canoe both Joanne and Nancy were rested, and hopeful that very soon they would again see those they best loved.

But once again moving rapidly down-stream they began to feel tired, and as the scout bent to his paddle and the river seemed to slide by them Joanne and Nancy ceased to chatter of their journey, and fell asleep.

The scout, from his place in the bow of the canoe, glanced over his shoulder now and then toward the sleeping girls. He knew he could have traveled more swiftly without them, but not for a moment had he even considered leaving them alone and helpless in the wilderness; and he smiled, remembering the valuable information that now rested so safely in Joanne's pocket. He might not, he well knew, have the good fortune to himself carry Red-bird's pouch to General Schuyler, but he told himself that these little maids would prove the best of messengers.

Neither Joanne nor Nancy ever forgot that journey down the Mohawk River to Albany. The first night they slept comfortably in a settler's cabin, and were off before sunrise the next morning. The second day was a day of hardship, for at various places the rapids in the river were too dangerous to attempt, and the scout

would lift the canoe on his shoulders, and followed by the two little girls, make his way
through underbrush or rocky pasture until a
smooth stretch of river made it again safe to paddle down the stream.

It was dusk at the second day when the canoe
came near Schenectady and slid rapidly past to
land a few miles below the town.

" I have friends near here who will give us a
lodging," the scout declared, as the canoe turned
into a little creek and they found themselves
landing at a narrow wharf and being led up a
path toward a square wooden house, the largest
house that Joanne or Nancy had ever seen.

The scout walked beside them, and just before
reaching the house he rested his hand on Joanne's
shoulder and said gravely:

" You tell me that your father is an American
soldier, stationed at Fort Stanwix! "

" Oh, yes, indeed! He was sent there but a
month since," replied Joanne.

" And you and this other little maid," and he
turned a glance toward Nancy, " have solemnly
promised me to deliver the Indian's wallet to
General Schuyler. Your father's life and safety,
the lives and safety of many settlers in the Mo-

hawk Valley, depend on that message reaching him."

" But do you not mean to give it to him yourself? " asked Joanne, a little fearful lest she and Nancy were to be again left to find their way on as best they might, but the scout's friendly words reassured her.

" That is as may be. I shall soon know. But you, little maids, need have no fear. In this house live loyal Americans who will befriend you and see that you reach your friends safely. Be not afraid," and he advanced toward the door and rapped loudly. The big door swung open and Joanne and Nancy saw a kindly-faced elderly woman gazing down at them as if too surprised to speak; but she had instantly put forth a welcoming hand to draw them into a large room well lighted by candles.

" Sit thee down," she said gently, leading them toward a broad settle, and sitting down with Joanne on one side of her and Nancy on the other, and nodding and smiling as the scout told her the story of finding the two little girls in the far-off forest, and of their journey down the Mohawk.

" You must send them on to Albany to-morrow, Mrs. Campbell. This little maid," and he touched Joanne's arm, " wears a ring given her by the Indian Brant. It saved her once and may again; but she has a grandmother in Albany who will welcome her."

CHAPTER X

TO ALBANY

NANCY and Joanne were quick to notice that "the scout"—they were never to know him by any other name—was very much at home in the big house where the kindly Mrs. Campbell now did her best to make the little girls comfortable.

After an excellent supper the scout again cautioned Joanne not to speak of Red-bird's pouch or the message it contained to anyone, and then bade them good-night.

Mrs. Campbell led the two tired little maids up a broad staircase to a big comfortable room where a cushiony bed seemed to Joanne the most beautiful thing she had seen since leaving home.

As Mrs. Campbell brought pitchers of hot water and soft towels of hand-woven linen she exclaimed over Nancy's tangled hair and the rents and slits in their torn skirts.

"I declare! There is but little left of your skirt save the pocket," she told Joanne. "I had best take it away. I can manage a skirt for you from one of mine."

But Joanne held tightly to the tattered gingham, refusing to let her new friend take it.

"If you please, ma'am, I will keep it, because of the pocket," she said. "May it not be that I could put a whole skirt over it?"

Mrs. Campbell, thinking it very likely that Joanne's pocket held some girlish treasure, smilingly agreed, and was amused to see Joanne roll up the skirt and put it carefully on a chair near the bed.

After the warm bath, and when Mrs. Campbell had combed and brushed their hair and provided them with nightgowns, she bade them good-night and the two little wanderers climbed into the big bed.

"It's as soft as clouds!" Nancy murmured sleepily. "Oh, Joanne, do you s'pose your Grandmother Clarke will have room for me in her house?"

"Of course she will!" Joanne promptly replied. "But, Nancy, I wish we had asked the scout to send word to our mothers that we are safe, and to ask my mother to please to come to Albany."

"We will ask him in the morning," Nancy responded sleepily.

But when morning came, and Mrs. Campbell appeared with more hot water, and bringing a skirt for Nancy made of golden brown linen, and one for Joanne of stout blue linsey-woolsey, as well as their stockings that she had washed and mended, she told them that the scout had gone. " It is a time when every American must do his utmost to protect the settlers from the invaders," she said; " but he bade me tell you that this very day he has sent word of your safety by a messenger bound up the river to Fort Stanwix; so 'twill not be long before your mothers will know that you are safe in Albany."

" Are we never to see the scout again? " questioned Joanne, a little anxiously; " he was most kind to us, and we have not thanked him."

Mrs. Campbell patted the little girl's shoulder approvingly. " 'Tis right to have a grateful spirit, my child; may it not be that you can do him a service in return! He tells me you must reach Albany as soon as may be; and Nicholas has the horse harnessed and waiting for you to have your breakfast and be off."

The hot porridge, the scrambled eggs, the waffles with new butter and honey, made a breakfast that Joanne and Nancy were sure could not be improved on; and when they had finished Mrs. Campbell said they must start at once, and the little girls noticed two broad-rimmed hats of plaited grass lying on the settle. One hat had a band and strings of a broad blue plaided ribbon, and this one Mrs. Campbell put on Joanne, tying the strings under the little girl's chin. The other hat was trimmed in the same manner only the ribbon was a pale yellow, and Nancy exclaimed admiringly as Mrs. Campbell bade her put it on.

" 'Twould not be seemly for two small maids to drive into Albany bareheaded. I made these hats last autumn, but have had no use for them; and last night I bethought me of the ribbons that have been useless for years, so I trimmed the hats!" and Mrs. Campbell nodded and smiled as if well pleased with the result of her handiwork, and Joanne and Nancy eagerly declared that the hats were lovely and that they were proud indeed to wear them.

"You must both come and make me a real visit," said Mrs. Campbell, after the two little girls had climbed into the back seat of the wagon, and had again thanked her for her goodness to them.

" Yes, indeed. We will come as soon as the British are sent away from Mohawk Valley!" Joanne promised, and the stout Nicholas, Mrs. Campbell's fourteen-year-old son, turned from his place in the front seat to say:

" The scout says the English and Brant's savages mean to capture Albany. But they'll more like be driven to Canada!"

" Let us hope it may be soon. And that we will be rid of British invasion forever," said Mrs. Campbell. " Now, Nicholas, drive carefully, and see to it that no harm befall these little maids! The basket of luncheon is under the back seat, and do not eat it until you have passed Cohoes Falls."

Nicholas promised soberly. Although only fourteen Nicholas Campbell had for the past year done his best to take his father's place in the work and duties of the large farm while Mr. Campbell was with the American Army, and the boy was quite sure that he could drive Joanne and Nancy safely to Albany.

" 'Tis but a matter of fifteen miles," he said, as the big gray horse trotted out of the yard and turned into the road leading to Albany. Tall oak and chestnut trees shaded the road for a time, and Joanne and Nancy were well pleased to be riding so comfortably. The wagon-seat had a high back for them to rest against, Nicholas had put in a long cricket for them to put their feet on, and rested and refreshed by the good food, the night in the comfortable bed, and comforted by the thought that their mothers would soon hear of their safety, the little girls now began to enjoy their adventure, thinking that this pleasant ride to Albany was but the beginning of good fortune.

They admired each other's hats and the skirts Mrs. Campbell had given them, and now and then Nicholas would turn and bid them look, as with his whip he pointed toward several deer grazing in a near-by meadow, or at a flock of wild pigeon hovering over a huge ledge. The road was rough, and Nicholas drove carefully; but he listened eagerly when Joanne told him the story of her meeting with Brant and showed him the silver ring.

" 'Tis right enough for a girl to wear it, with savages lurking everywhere; but I'd not be beholden to Joseph Brant: for all his education he is but a cruel Indian," Nicholas declared, and at this Joanne and Nancy looked at each other in amazement, as both the little girls had regarded the silver ring as a valuable possession.

"But when Red-bird, the Indian who took us through the forest, saw it he was more friendly. He might even have scalped us had not Joanne worn it!" said Nancy. "Surely, 'tis a good thing that Brant gave it to Joanne?" and Nancy leaned forward on the wide seat to look eagerly at their young driver, who now shook his head soberly, and repeated:

"I wouldn't wear his ring!"

Joanne felt her face flush uncomfortably: she had been very proud that the Indian chief had praised her courage, and had believed the ring valuable as a proof of his protection, and now this boy was sneering at it: talking as if it were almost a disgrace to accept safety from such a one as Brant. And now she leaned forward and said angrily: "I guess I'm just as brave as any boy! I'm as brave as you are, Nicholas Campbell."

The boy looked around and smiled good-naturedly. "Maybe," he answered teasingly, "but I don't wear the ring of a traitor to protect me!"

"Well, then, neither do I!" exclaimed Joanne,

pulling off the silver ring and throwing it into the underbrush. " There it goes! " she added.

Nicholas' smile vanished, and he drew rein so sharply that the gray horse nearly stumbled.

" 'Tis like looking for a needle in a haystack," he said, as he jumped to the ground, " but I'll fasten General and look for it," and taking a halter from under the seat he fastened the surprised " General " to a near-by tree, and turned in the direction where the ring had vanished.

" I don't want it back! " Joanne called after him. " I won't wear it. I guess I can be brave enough without an old silver ring! "

Nancy's blue eyes stared at Joanne reproachfully. " Oh, Joanne! What ever made you throw it away? Why, we might even meet Indians before we reach Albany. What ever made you do it? "

" That boy! " replied Joanne; " as if girls were not just as brave as he is."

" But he's nearly grown up," said Nancy. " Of course he's braver than a little girl! "

" He's bigger, but I am just as brave," persisted Joanne.

Nicholas came back smiling, and held out the little shining ring.

" 'Tis wonderful indeed. It caught on a shrub and hung as if waiting to be picked," he said, holding the ring toward Joanne. " Put it on, little maid; we'll say no more of courage, and you had best wear it."

" You said 'twas a traitor's ring," Joanne answered. " I do not want it."

" I'll keep it then until we get to Albany; maybe you'll change your mind," the boy said, slipping the ring into his pocket and climbing again to his seat, while Joanne, wishing it were possible to prove that very moment that she was as brave as Nicholas, turned her head away from Nancy's reproachful gaze, and wished the gray horse would go at a faster pace that they might reach Albany and see no more of this tall boy who sat on the front seat with Brant's silver ring in his pocket. Joanne could feel the deerskin pouch with its important message resting safely in the pocket of the ragged skirt, over which she wore the one Mrs. Campbell had given her, and for a moment the little girl was tempted to exclaim that the scout had believed her brave enough to carry an important message to General Philip Schuyler. She might even have done this had not Nicholas just then turned the gray horse into an opening among the forest trees that bordered the rough highway and said:

"This is where my mother takes the noonday rest when we journey to Albany. 'Tis a pleasant place, with a spring of cool water near by."

It was indeed a pleasant place. The tall pine trees shaded a small clearing where a little spring bubbled up from a bed of green moss. The ground was thickly carpeted with pine-spills, and an old log, thickly cushioned with moss as if made for a seat, rested near the spring.

Nicholas helped the little girls from the wagon, drew out the luncheon basket and set it near the log, and then turned to make "General" comfortable, while Joanne and Nancy opened the basket.

"It's lovely here; it's lovely to ride to Albany, instead of being all cramped up in a canoe!" exclaimed Nancy, taking off her hat and laying it carefully on the log, and Joanne's face lost its sulky look as she drew from the basket sandwiches, boiled eggs, a meat pie, and appetizing spiced cookies, a jar of jelly, and flaky turnovers.

"'Tis like a birthday feast, is it not, Nancy?" she declared. "If our mothers and Lucy could

see us they would think we were indeed fortunate."

" And it was Lucy, after all, who started us on
this journey," said Nancy thoughtfully.

CHAPTER XI

JOANNE DISAPPEARS

NICHOLAS brought cool water from the spring, and did his best to be helpful and to have his young guests enjoy the excellent luncheon his mother had provided for them. Joanne noticed that he was dressed very much as the " scout " had been, only that he wore a blue flannel hunting shirt instead of a tunic of deerskin, and his cap was also of blue cloth.

Both the girls had for some time heard a distant roar, that, but for the clear sky and soft air, they would have thought was distant thunder, and Nancy now held up her hand and said:

" That roaring sound is louder than ever here. What is it? " and she turned toward Nicholas.

" Cohoes Falls," he replied. " 'Tis a mile behind us, and had we plenty of time I would have turned from the highway that you might see it. But I must get back to the farm as early as may be."

" But will you not stay the night in Albany?

94

I know surely that my Grandmother Clarke would be well pleased to have you," said Joanne.

Nicholas shook his head. "My mother bade me rest old General an hour in Albany and drive back. I mean to be home ere dark," he replied, and then again told of the height of Cohoes Falls where the Mohawk River plunges over the rock.

"Why, you can hardly hear yourself speak when you are near it, and it sends up a silvery spray as white as wool, and the whirlpools below are blue and green."

"Maybe we can see it on our journey home," suggested Joanne. But Nicholas made no response to this, for he knew that it was the plan of General Burgoyne to sweep from Canada through the Mohawk Valley, and who could tell if any cabin of loyal Americans would remain?

As soon as luncheon was over they started on, and as they neared Albany Nicholas bade them remember that now the Mohawk River had joined with the Hudson, and very soon both the little girls were exclaiming over the houses built of brick set so nearly together; of shops whose windows displayed many things that Joanne and Nancy had never before seen, and when Nicholas said:

"Just ahead you can plainly see St. Peter's Church! Did you not say your grandmother's house was near by?" and turned a questioning glance toward Joanne, she answered eagerly:

"Yes! Yes! And I am sure anyone can tell you, for my father has often said 'twas one of the finest houses in Albany."

"Maybe this is it," said Nancy, as they passed the stone church and drew near to a square house of red brick with a pillared porch. There were broad seats on each side of the porch, and on one of these sat an elderly lady. She wore a lilac colored gown, and a white cap, and she was knitting busily.

Nicholas brought General to a standstill and, removing his cap, called: "Madame, will you be so kind as to direct me to the house of Madame Penelope Clarke?"

The old lady looked up from her work and nodded smilingly.

"That I will, young sir, if you will tell me ——"

But even as she spoke Joanne had begun to scramble down from the cart and now was standing directly in front of the old lady saying:

"Grandmother Clarke! If you please, I am Joanne!"

For a moment Madame Clarke stared at the little girl and then her knitting fell to the floor and she reached out her arms to Joanne exclaiming: "It is indeed Joanne," and then began asking questions.

Nicholas had helped Nancy from the wagon, and was just climbing back to his seat when Madame Clarke called to him:

"Be not in such haste to depart, young sir. Take your horse through the driveway here to the stable, and then return," and Nicholas, making a clumsy bow, turned General in to the driveway toward which Madame Clarke had pointed, while she drew Joanne and Nancy into the house, and Joanne hurriedly told the story of their journey down the river from the cabin in Mohawk Valley.

"And, if you please, Grandmother, where does General Philip Schuyler live?" she concluded.

"General Philip Schuyler? Why, child, he has but returned from the Congress in Philadelphia, and is at his fine house across the ferry. What do you so wish to know of him?" replied Mrs. Clarke, a little amused that Joanne should speak so earnestly of the commander of the Northern forces of the American Army.

"I wish to see him," replied Joanne.

"Well, that is but natural, dear child," replied Mrs. Clarke. "It was but yesterday that all Albany turned out to welcome him and to do him honor. He deserves well of his townsmen. He is a friend of General Washington's, and Albany is very proud of him."

"Is it a long way to his house, Grandma?" questioned Joanne. Before Mrs. Clarke could reply Nancy exclaimed:

"Joanne has a message for him. It is in her pocket. The scout ——"

But before she could say another word Nancy found her mouth tightly covered by Joanne's hands, that, struggle as she might, she could not escape from.

"Joanne! Children! What is all this? Joanne, let go Nancy this moment!" commanded the astonished Mrs. Clarke, but Joanne, standing behind Nancy with both hands firmly clasped over Nancy's mouth, shook her head.

"Not until Nancy promises—she knows what!" she answered.

"'Promise'! How can the girl speak! Obey

me, Joanne! " and Madame Clarke firmly seized Joanne's hands and drew them away from Nancy's struggling head.

" I won't promise, Joanne Clarke! " she angrily declared, and the astonished Nicholas who had just entered the room stared in amazement to see Joanne and Nancy facing each other as if they were sworn enemies.

But Grandma Clarke held Joanne firmly with one arm, and rested her other hand on Nancy's shoulder, and welcomed Nicholas with a smile.

" These little maids tell me you must start home within an hour, young sir," she said, " and I bade my servant set forth some small refreshment for you in the dining-room. If you will kindly open the door next the window and step in I will soon join you."

Nicholas bowed again, and as he turned toward the door he wondered if he had been mistaken in thinking that Joanne and Nancy had quarreled.

" I must see to it the little maid has her silver ring," he thought, as a smiling colored woman motioned him to a seat at a well-spread table.

In the meantime Madame Clarke led the two little girls to an upper chamber, where to their surprise they found spread out on the bed two dresses of stout home-made white linen, two complete sets of underwear trimmed with hand-knit lace, two pairs of open-work cotton stockings, and resting on the floor beside the bed stood two pairs of kid slippers with buckles of shining silver.

" Julie will come up and help you dress in a moment," said Mrs. Clarke; " but first of all tell me what is all this about a message for General Philip Schuyler? " and she looked first at Nancy and then at Joanne.

" If you please, Grandmother Clarke, may I wait until to-morrow to tell you? " asked Joanne, and to this her grandmother promptly agreed, thinking it some girlish secret of small consequence.

" I will step down to the dining-room and thank young Nicholas for bringing you to Albany, and as soon as Julie has made you tidy do you also come down," she said, and with a light kiss on Joanne's flushed cheek she left the girls to themselves, quite sure they would speedily make friends again, and smiling a little over Joanne's eagerness to see General Schuyler. Not for a moment did Grandmother Clarke imagine that the " message " of which Nancy had spoken was of any consequence, although in

June, 1777, the residents of Albany well knew that the British planned to move down the Mohawk Valley and capture the American forces at the forts on the frontier. Fort Stanwix, where Joanne's father was stationed, was one of these. But Joanne's grandmother imagined that her young visitors had some girlish secret, and hoped they would not again quarrel in regard to it, so she went down to make sure that young Nicholas Campbell was being properly served.

The moment Madame Clarke left the chamber Joanne faced Nancy and angrily exclaimed: "Well! Nancy Wagner! After promising the scout not to tell of Red-bird's wallet I should think you'd be ashamed!"

"*I* didn't promise, and I am not ashamed!" declared Nancy. "And how are you ever going to find General Schuyler unless your grandmother goes with you?" Then, as her eyes rested on the pretty garments spread out on the bed Nancy forgot for the moment all her troubles and said: "Joanne, do look at the lovely dresses, the fine stockings and the pretty shoes! Where did your grandma get them so quickly?"

Joanne shook her head, and was about to say more of Nancy's disloyalty when a rap at the door was quickly followed by the entrance of the smiling Julie.

" If yo' please, Mistress Clarke say I am to help yo'," she announced in her soft pleasant voice. In 1777 black people were held as slaves in New York, and considered themselves as a part of the family they served.

Both Joanne and Nancy were at first a little shy of this good-natured woman who, talking steadily, began to help Nancy take off her dress, urging the little girls to hurry, as Mistress Clarke wished them to come down-stairs.

" Dese yar t'ings on de bed belonged to Miss Clarissa w'en she were 'bout yo' age," said Julie nodding toward Joanne, " an' her ma save 'em up!"

" My Aunt Clarissa, who lives in New York?" questioned Joanne.

" Yas, Miss Clarissa marry a gran' English officer and lib in a gran' house!" responded Julie.

Nancy admired every garment that Julie held up for her inspection, and for a moment neither of them noticed Joanne who stood by the window looking out toward the gray stone church. As she looked out Joanne noticed a shining vane shaped like a horse on the top of the house opposite, and further down the street a figure of a golden goose seemed to float in the air over a large mansion, and the little girl's thoughts sped back to her cabin home. Wonderful as it was to be in the fine city of Albany Joanne now sharply realized that she was homesick. She thought longingly of her mother, and for a second seemed to again behold the silvery fairy who had visited her at her playhouse.

Joanne looked over her shoulder at Nancy and Julie, who were laughing and talking over the dainty garments, and Joanne made the resolve that she would not wait another moment before starting to find General Schuyler and give him the deerskin pouch that held the letter intended for Burgoyne. " And then I will ask my grandmother to find a way for me to go straight home. Maybe I could start to-morrow," she thought, as she tiptoed noiselessly across the room, sped down the stairs and through the open door.

" Of course anyone can tell me where General Philip Schuyler lives," she whispered to herself, as she ran down the street.

Joanne could hardly have reached the porch when Julie exclaimed: " Whar de mistress's lille gran'-gal gone to? " and sent a searching glance around the room expecting to see Joanne appear.

" I guess she didn't want to change her dress," said Nancy who was admiring herself in the white dress and wishing that Lucy could see the shining buckles on her pretty slippers. " Joanne's prob'ly gone down-stairs so Nicholas will not forget to give her the silver ring," she added, and then told Julie the story of Joanne's meeting with the Indian Brant, and of his giving his ring to the little maid of Mohawk Valley.

Before Nancy had quite finished, Madame Clarke appeared at the door.

" Nicholas is ready to start, and waiting to bid you good-bye," she said, and glancing quickly around the room added:

" Where is Joanne? "

CHAPTER XII

GENERAL SCHUYLER AND JOANNE

IN spite of Joanne's eagerness to fulfil her promise to the scout and deliver Red-bird's pouch to General Philip Schuyler as soon as possible, she nearly forgot her errand as she heard Albany's town clock peal forth, and she stood quite still counting: " One, two, three, four! " and looked about wondering where the sounds came from and admiring the broad street with the neat houses and flower beds.

A number of passers-by stared curiously at the little girl in the queer skirt and moccasins who stood bareheaded in front of St. Peter's Church counting the strokes of the town clock; and two girls of about Joanne's own age stopped on the other side of the street and watched her, asking each other where a girl dressed in so strange a way could have come from; for these girls had never been out of Albany, and their own dresses were of silk or muslin or of the finest cloth brought from France. Janet Wendell, the

taller of the two, on this pleasant June day wore
a dress of white India muslin with many tiny
ruffles on the full skirt, her scoop-shaped hat was
trimmed with white ribbons, and her stockings
were of silk, her shoes of shining patent leather,
while her hands were nearly covered by white
silk mitts. Molly Van Corlear, her companion,
wore a dress of pale blue flowered silk with a
close shirred hat of the same material and carried
a tiny parasol of a deeper shade of blue, so that
no greater contrast could be imagined than that
between Joanne's rough dress and the costumes
of the two girls who stood watching her.

"Do you suppose she is lost, Janet?" questioned Molly. "May it not be that she is a country child from the Mohawk Valley who has wandered away from her parents?" and Molly's face
grew a little anxious and pitiful at the very
thought of being separated from one's father and
mother.

Janet gave her companion a scornful glance
as she replied: "Of course she's country, stupid!
Do Albany girls run about bareheaded with their
hair like that," and she pointed toward the rough-
ened braid of Joanne's hair, "and old Indian
moccasins? I'll wager she's the child of some of

the Mohawk Valley settlers who have come to Albany to be safe from the Tories and Indians. She seems going the same way we go;" for Joanne was now walking on at a brisk pace, looking anxiously at every passer-by as if wishing to question them, and at last her glance fell on the two little girls and she instantly made up her mind to ask them to help her find General Schuyler and ran across the street toward them.

"Will you be so kind as to tell me the nearest way to the house of General Philip Schuyler?" she asked, with her friendly smile, thinking how pretty the two girls were and admiring their beautiful dresses.

"The house of General Schuyler," Janet said stiffly, "is a good half-mile from here; you cross a ferry to reach it," and she would have walked on had not Molly exclaimed:

"We ourselves are bound straight to General Schuyler's house; our mothers are to join us at the ferry. Will you not come with us?" and the kindly little girl gave Joanne so pleasant a smile that Janet's frown deepened, and she said:

"Do you forget, Molly, that Mistress Schuyler is giving a party? It may well be this girl

would not wish to intrude on a party, and if so
be she has an errand, will do it on some other
day!" and again Janet started forward.

Joanne's face flushed angrily.

" My errand is with General Schuyler, and I
will be welcome," she declared, and would have
hurried on had not Molly's hand in its mitt of
blue knitted silk clasped her own, and Molly's
friendly voice said:

" It may be that General Schuyler is not at
home but has already gone to Fort Edward; but
you had best come with us and find out, then
you can tell your parents that you did the errand."

For a moment Joanne did not reply but
walked on beside her new friend, while Janet
kept well in advance of them. Joanne was now a
little puzzled as to the course to follow, but at
last said thoughtfully:

" I'll have to find him."

" Maybe he is at home," Molly responded
hopefully, and the two girls walked on together.
Now and then Janet would turn and look scorn-
fully at Molly, and as they neared the ferry and
could see a group of ladies and children in pretty
summer dresses awaiting the ferry-boat, Janet

turned and faced Molly and Joanne and exclaimed:

"Molly Van Corlear! Let this Mohawk Valley maid do her own errands. Do you mean to
take her with us to the very door of the Schuyler
mansion? She looks but little better than an Indian!" and Janet's black eyes shone angrily upon
this undesired companion, and Joanne now realized the difference in her appearance from these
girls in their dainty gowns and shining shoes, and
her own generous nature prompted her to say
quickly:

"Indeed I do not look nearly as fine as do
most of the Indian girls. And I am not meaning to trouble anyone. I thank you for so kindly
letting me walk beside you to the ferry," and
smiling at Molly, Joanne sped past the astonished Janet and ran toward the ferry-boat that
was now at the landing-place and was the first
one on board.

"Don't you dare let anyone know that we
brought that girl to the ferry, Molly Van Corlear!" Janet whispered angrily, as they walked
toward the group.

No one seemed to notice Joanne on the boat;
the ferryman took it for granted that the queerly-

dressed child came with the others, especially as
little Molly Van Corlear had slipped the pennies
for the strange little girl's ferriage into his hand
with the whispered words: " She's going to the
Schuyler mansion."

As the boat landed and the passengers made
their way up to the stately house Joanne followed silently. Now and then Molly would look
back at her and nod encouragingly, and Joanne
told herself that Molly Van Corlear was the
loveliest and kindest girl in all the world, and
she wished there was something she could do for
Molly.

Mistress Schuyler and her young daughter
Elizabeth, and several others of the Schuyler
family were gathered on the porch to welcome
their guests, and now Molly slipped away from
her friends and joined Joanne.

" If you will tell me your name I will present
you to Madame Schuyler and you can ask for
the General," she said, with her pretty smile that
made dimples show at each side of her mouth.

Joanne's face showed how greatly she appre-
ciated Molly's kindness, but she hesitated to tell
her name, remembering that her untidy appearance would be of but little credit to her Grand-

mother Clarke who was, very likely, well known to these people, so she thanked Molly and said:

" I am a little maid from Mohawk Valley, with a message for General Schuyler."

But before Molly and Joanne reached the steps, two mounted soldiers trotted down the driveway and behind them, on a fine bay horse, came General Schuyler himself, and Molly exclaimed: " There he is! Right here! " and curtseyed so suddenly that she nearly lost her balance as she saw Joanne run forward calling:

" General Schuyler! General Schuyler! "

General Schuyler promptly drew rein. He had little daughters of his own about the age of this wild-looking maid who was so dangerously near the heels of his spirited horse, and he was puzzled to know what the child might want, for never before had any of the children of Albany forgotten to approach him with due respect and deference and he now looked down a little sternly as he asked: " What is it, little maid? " while the two soldiers turned their horses and waited as if expecting some unknown danger.

Joanne, fumbling for the pocket in her ragged skirt, now drew out the beaded pouch and held it up toward the General, saying hurriedly:

" If you please, sir, a scout from Fort Stanwix bade me give you this. 'Twas lost by one of Brant's Indians, and 'tis of importance."

Reaching down the General took the pouch from the upstretched hand, opened it, unfolded the paper it contained, and gravely read the message that had been intended for the English General Burgoyne.

" Who are you, child? " he asked, and Joanne told him her name and added:

" I am the granddaughter of Mistress Clarke, who lives not far from St. Peter's Church, and she would be ill pleased to see me so poorly dressed."

A kindly smile flashed over the General's dark handsome countenance as he quickly responded:

" Mistress Clarke will, if I mistake not, be well pleased to know how great a service her little granddaughter has rendered to the cause of America's liberties. We shall meet again, little maid," and with a smiling nod he rode on.

Joanne, looking after him for a moment, now realized that she was standing alone on the driveway. Molly Van Corlear and the handsome, disagreeable Janet Wendell had disappeared. She glanced back toward the mansion whose doors and windows stood invitingly open, and then with a little sigh at the thought that she might not again see the kind Molly, Joanne started toward the ferry. She had nearly reached the shore when she saw a tall boy running up from the landing, and called out:

" Nicholas! Nicholas Campbell."

" And a nice hunt you've given me!" exclaimed the good-natured Nicholas. " Had it not been that Nancy told us you were bound to find General Schuyler we'd not known where to look for you. And 'tis now six; I'll not get home 'til well on to midnight. But come now, the horse is on the other side of the ferry and I'll take you to your grandmother. 'Tis plain enough you are fated to be lost if you are out of sight of your friends."

" But see how quickly I am found!" replied Joanne happily, feeling now that her worries were safely over. " I must go to my truly home as soon as I can," she added thoughtfully. " I like not for my mother to be alone in that far-off cabin."

" Your silver ring would be of use to you in that wild country," said Nicholas. " I doubt not I'd be glad to wear it myself if I lived so far from forts," and drawing the ring from his pocket he held it out for Joanne to take, adding: "And I was but teasing you, little maid, when I questioned your courage, and I am sorry for it."

Joanne took the ring soberly and without a word placed it on her finger. She well knew that the protection of the chief of the Mohawks might mean her mother's safety and her own, and she was glad indeed to again wear the silver ring.

CHAPTER XIII

JOANNE FINDS A NEW FRIEND

ALTHOUGH Nancy had told Madame Clarke that Joanne " had prob'ly gone to find General Schuyler," Joanne's grandmother had no idea that her little granddaughter was the bearer of news that was, perhaps, to save the valley of the Mohawk from being conquered by the Tories and their Indian allies, but decided that Joanne must be a very thoughtless and wilful child; so that as Nicholas led the little girl up the steps saying: " She found her way straight to General Schuyler," as if expecting Madame Clarke would be well pleased, she only responded gravely:

" I am indeed sorry, Nicholas, that you have had the trouble and delay of finding her," and hardly seemed to notice that Joanne's glance was fixed pleadingly upon her grandmother's grave face.

Nicholas bade them all a smiling good-bye and started his horse off at a rapid pace. He well knew with what anxiety his mother would watch for his return and was eager to be on his way.

Madame Clarke led the little girls indoors, and bade Nancy enter the front room, saying: "Amuse yourself by looking out of the window until Joanne and I return," and then bade Joanne follow her to the upper chamber, where Julie promptly appeared, ready to help the little girl change her worn clothing for the dainty garments her grandmother had provided.

"When you are ready, Joanne, Julie will bring you to the dining-room," then, turning to Julie, Madame Clarke added: "And do not for one moment, Julie, let Joanne out of your sight. I fear she is not to be trusted alone," and without even a glance toward the shamed and astonished Joanne, who had been well pleased that she had so carefully obeyed the scout, Madame Clarke left the room.

It was hard work for Joanne to keep back the tears as the kindly Julie bathed her flushed face, brushed out her pretty wavy hair and tied it with a rose-colored ribbon, and then helped the little girl dress declaring:

"Dar! Yo' looks jes' like a rose yerse'f, honey. Yo' does so. An' yo' shu' be de spitten image of Miss Clarissa w'en she were 'bout yo' size," and Julie smiled and nodded approvingly; but Joanne was thinking longingly of her mother, of the far-off cabin in Mohawk Valley, and resolving to go home as soon as she possibly could; but when her grandmother returned the little girl was ready to go down-stairs and Madame Clarke gave a little start of surprise as she, too, noticed Joanne's resemblance to her daughter Clarissa, and she smiled at the little girl more kindly as she said:

" It is indeed good fortune that I have kept the clothing your Aunt Clarissa wore when she was your age, and you remind me of her," and Grandma Clarke for the moment forgot that Joanne had caused her needless anxiety.

" If you please, Grandma, I want to go home," Joanne faltered, looking down at her pretty slippers whose square buckles gleamed in the light of the tall candle set in sconces on the wall above the broad stairway; before Mrs. Clarke could respond Nancy came running toward them exclaiming:

" A soldier has just ridden up to this house ——" and at that moment there was a loud knock on the outer door and Julie hastened to open it, and Joanne heard the soldier ask:

" Is this the residence of Madame Clarke who has a small granddaughter just arrived from Mohawk Valley? " and felt her grandmother's clasp tighten on her hand as Mrs. Clarke stepped forward saying:

" I am Madame Clarke, and this is my little granddaughter. What is your errand? "

The young soldier touched his cap and bowed. " General Philip Schuyler presents his compliments to Madame Clarke, and if it be convenient to her he will give himself the pleasure of calling upon her within the hour."

" Say to General Schuyler that Madame Clarke will indeed be honored by his visit," she responded, and with another bow the young soldier turned back to his horse, mounted and galloped down the street.

For a moment the little group stood in the doorway looking after him, and then, with a little sigh, Mrs. Clarke said:

" I know not on what errand the General comes. He has but little time in these sad days for a friendly visit. What did he say to you, child? " and she turned toward Joanne.

" If you please, Grandma, he did but say I had been of service and that you would be proud of me," said Joanne, her voice trembling a little.

" Well, 'tis a time of strange happenings; and I am well disposed toward the opinions of General Schuyler; and now, Julie, see that these little maids have their supper," said Madame Clarke, and Nancy and Joanne were both quite ready to follow Julie to the dining-room.

" Oh, Joanne! Is it not wonderful to have solid silver spoons, and to live in this grand house? Are you not glad the scout brought us here? And what do you suppose Mother and Lucy will say when they reach Albany and find me dressed like this!" and Nancy endeavored to see her own back by looking over her shoulder.

" Maybe you won't ever see Lucy again; maybe she was lost, and wandered off in the woods, and ——" but Joanne's mournful remarks were sharply interrupted by a wail from Nancy, who looked at Joanne with so woeful a face that Joanne promptly declared she had only been trying to tease her, and that of course Lucy was safe and sound, and by this time well on the way toward Albany with her father and mother.

As the two girls talked Julie served them to

hot chocolate, small biscuit brought fresh from the oven, slices of cold chicken, and bade them help themselves from the glass dish of grape jelly and the plate of sugar cookies.

They had nearly finished supper when Joanne said: " I want to go home, Nancy. I must. My mother is all alone, and 'tis not safe for her."

" But maybe she will come to Albany now you are here; and anyway you could not protect her," replied Nancy.

Joanne shook her head. " No, my mother will not leave home. There is the little cow, and Billy, our horse, and the chickens. Mother will not let them be hurt, and she will be glad that I am safe in Albany. But I *could* protect her, Nancy Wagner! White men would not harm her, and have I not Brant's ring so that the Indians will be friendly? " and Joanne held out her hand and Nancy saw the gleam of the silver ring on her friend's thumb, and at that moment both the little girls heard the sound of the big brass knocker and whispered in unison: " General Schuyler! " and slipped from their chairs and stood close together wondering on what errand the commander of the Northern division of the American Army had come; and it was not long

She Now Curtseyed Very Prettily

before Julie, who had hastened to open the door for Madame Clarke's distinguished visitor, again entered the dining-room and smilingly announced:

" Miss Joanne, yo' gran'ma say yo' are to come wid me to see de Gen'ral! "

" Am I not to come? " asked Nancy, but Julie shook her head.

" Not'in' were said 'bout yo' comin', Missy, so I reckon yo' better not," responded the smiling Julie, leading Joanne from the room, while Nancy, deciding to have another cooky, returned to the table.

The parlor door stood open and Joanne's grandmother, flushed and smiling as if she had just been hearing the best of good news, came forward to meet her little granddaughter who, happily remembering that her mother had often told her that a little girl should always curtsey in entering a room where there were older people, now curtseyed very prettily, and stood looking first at the tall, smiling General and then at her grandmother, and Madame Clarke was the first to speak.

" Joanne, General Schuyler wishes you to tell him of the scout who found you and Nancy in the forest," she said, leading the little girl across the room; and sitting on the broad sofa beside General Schuyler Joanne answered his questions regarding her discovery of the Indian's beaded pouch, and described the friendly scout who had brought the two little girls to the Campbells' home.

As she concluded the story Joanne said: " I guess the reason the Indian did not scalp us was because I showed him the ring Brant gave me."

" Brant! Joseph Brant, who has joined forces with the British to capture the American Army?" questioned General Schuyler.

" Yes, sir," and Joanne repeated the story of her meeting with the Indian chief, and that he had told her that to be brave was half the battle.

" 'Tis more than half," declared General Schuyler; " but I am glad you have the ring. Here in Albany we are in safety, at least for the present, but in the Mohawk Valley no settler can be sure that he may not be captured by the Tories or their Indian allies. I am to-morrow sending a messenger to General Nicholas Herkimer with the message this little maid brought me, that he may know the need of calling in more troops to protect our frontiers."

General Schuyler now rose, evidently to take his departure, and as he smiled down at Joanne he said:

" Perhaps we may not meet again for some time, little maid, and so is there not some wish of yours that I can now grant in return for the service you have done me?" and greatly to Madame Clarke's dismay she heard Joanne eagerly exclaim:

" Oh, yes, yes! Please may I not go with your messenger to General Herkimer? 'Twill not be far from my home, and I must take care of my mother!"

General Schuyler looked questioningly toward Madame Clarke, but before her grandmother could speak Joanne was earnestly pleading to be allowed to accompany the messenger to General Herkimer, and when she finished her grandmother said:

" If it be not too much to ask, General Schuyler, I believe it may be well for Joanne to be with her mother until this great danger that threatens the liberties and safety of American homes be forever ended. It may indeed prove that the ring of the Indian Brant will protect Joanne and her mother."

General Schuyler promptly agreed. His messenger was a man to be trusted, a skilled scout and woodsman, he said; and after a few suggestions as to the preparations it would be wise to make for the girl's journey, he bade them farewell.

On the following day General Schuyler was to go to Fort Ticonderoga, and Joanne was not to see him again until she was a young lady and came to make her home in Albany, and was often a visitor at the Schuyler mansion.

After the departure of General Schuyler Grandma Clarke put her arm about Joanne and said:

"Why, I am as proud as if I had myself won a great battle. General Schuyler declared that by your coming straight to him the message is in time to be of the greatest help to the Americans in Mohawk Valley. You are a brave girl, my dear," and Joanne smiled back at her grandmother thinking herself a very fortunate girl.

CHAPTER XIV

UP THE MOHAWK VALLEY

THERE were many things for Joanne and Nancy to talk over that night, and, although Grandma Clarke had sent them to bed at an early hour, the little girls lay long awake, whispering over the possibilities of the journey that Joanne was to begin the next morning.

"It may be we will meet your father and mother and Lucy on our way and can tell them where you are, Nancy," said Joanne, and Nancy agreed that such a meeting would indeed be fortunate; and when she heard Joanne's story of her encounter with Molly Van Corlear and Janet Wendell, of Molly's friendly help and Janet's scornful behavior toward an ill-dressed little girl who needed a friend, Nancy again declared that it was a shame for Joanne to go away from Albany.

"Oh, Joanne! If you were only to stay here in your grandma's fine house that old Janet would soon find out that you were a friend of General Schuyler's, and that you had as pretty dresses as any girl in Albany! Why, Joanne!
125

Julie says there are drawers filled with clothes that your Aunt Clarissa used to wear," and for a moment Nancy forgot all about Janet's hateful behavior in recalling all Julie had told her of leghorn hats trimmed with roses, of embroidered silk capes, and of a dainty dress of rose-colored India mull.

But Joanne's eager whisper: " Nancy, I want you to do something for me, will you? " brought the little girl back to the fact that on the next day Joanne would be far away, and who could tell when they would meet again? —and she answered eagerly:

" Of course I will, Joanne."

" It's Molly! Oh, Nancy, just think of her being so good to a girl who looked the way I did! Why, she didn't seem to think anything about my old moccasins, or my being bareheaded or anything except that she could help me. Nancy," and Joanne nearly forgot to whisper in her earnestness, " Molly Van Corlear is 'most an angel! "

" What you want me to do? " Nancy reminded her, and with a little sigh Joanne went on:

" I want you to get acquainted with her. Grandma will know how to do it, and every time you see Molly, now remember, Nancy, *every* time, I want you to talk about me, and you tell Molly how pretty I think she is and how kind. And, Nancy, maybe you'd better tell her what Brant said about my being brave! Nancy! You're asleep!" and Joanne was tempted to awaken her companion but drowsily drifted off into thoughts of soon being once more at home, and it was not until the June sunlight streamed into the pleasant chamber that she awoke to find Julie just entering the room.

" Break'us' all waitin', honey," she whispered, " an' yo' jus' slip out ob bed quiet an' come in yo' grandma's room, an' not wake up Missy Nancy," and Joanne silently obeyed, although there were many things she wanted to say to Nancy, and she felt sober and a little sad to go away without bidding her good-bye.

But Grandma Clarke did not give Joanne time to speak of Nancy, for she bade the little girl dress as quickly as possible, and Joanne was surprised to find that she was to wear an entirely new set of garments, with the exception of her old moccasins; these, Grandma declared, were better suited to her journey than the shiny buckled slippers. The dress that Joanne was to wear was a simple straight garment of stout brown home-made linen. It was nearly the same color as her hair, and the cotton stockings were of the same shade; and when Joanne was dressed Grandma held up a little hat also made of brown linen, with strings that could be tied under her chin; and last of all there was a long cape of brown homespun which Mrs. Clarke folded into a neat package, saying: "June weather is uncertain, and it may well be that you'll welcome this cape. 'Tis a pity, dear child, you cannot take home all the clothing I have saved for you, but it may be I can get it to you before long, or that your mother will bring you to Albany," and then Joanne was hurried to the dining-room and had just eaten the last spoonful of her porridge when the clatter of horses' feet was heard on the street and Grandma Clarke exclaimed:

"Here is General Schuyler's messenger!" and Joanne jumped up from the table and ran to the window. Looking out she saw a big brown horse that was apparently trying to stand first on its hind feet, and then to dance sideways until its rider with a sharp word brought the animal to a standstill directly in front of the open window.

"Mercy on us! I do not know that it is safe

to let a little girl ride on so spirited a horse," said Madame Clarke, but Joanne had already tied the strings of her hat and taken up the small package that Julie had made ready for her.

"But I must go, Grandmother," she said soberly, and Grandmother nodded, and said:

"Yes, dear child, I suppose you must," and hand in hand the elderly woman and the little girl went to the porch and down the steps to where the brown horse stood as quietly as a lamb.

"Why, Jan Nellis!" exclaimed Madame Clarke, as she recognized the smiling young man who stood bowing to her beside his horse. "This is indeed good fortune. Joanne," she continued, "this is Master Jan Nellis, a friend of mine, who will take you safely home," and Joanne curtseyed and then found herself lifted to the back of the tall horse with Jan seated in front of her, and her bundle swinging from the saddle-bow.

Jan had given Grandma and Joanne no time for good-byes, and all they could do was to call to each other as Joanne clutched at the flannel blouse of her companion and the big horse swung rapidly off down the street.

Past the church, through the square, past the houses whose glittering weather-vanes, shaped like lions, geese, and even a sloop under full sail, Joanne had but yesterday admired and wondered at, and soon the big horse had left Albany behind and entered the road that would lead them to the Mohawk Valley.

Beyond an occasional word of warning to "Hold tight, little maid," as they galloped swiftly around a turn in the road, or a caution to look out for the sweep of wayside branches as their way narrowed, Joanne's companion had not spoken until they were well out in the country; but as they rode up a slope covered with thickly growing pines, he began to sing:

> "Now while blossoms take my sight,
>   With all the colors of delight;
>   While silver waters glide along,
>   To please my eye and court my song,
>   I'll lift my voice and tune my string,
>   And happily of freedom sing."

Joanne listened, thinking that if only Nancy could be riding beside her, and if she could hope to again see kind Molly Van Corlear, this ride would be a fine excursion, when her thoughts were interrupted by Jan's pleasant voice asking:

"And what do you think, little maid, of all this warfare? Even a little girl like you must know that Americans are fighting only for the safety of their homes. If we can but make the English know that though we will resist oppression we will never oppress," he added, as if thinking aloud, and Joanne hardly knew what to say in response, but announced:

" My father is at Fort Stanwix."

" Stanwix? Well, it has been renamed Schuyler, but the old name does as well, and I doubt not the old fort will put up a good defense if the Tories and their Indian allies attack it. Colonel Gansevoort is there doing his best to repair the fort, and every day brings nearer the time the English General Burgoyne will move toward Ticonderoga and send General St. Leger against Stanwix," said Jan, and then again hummed the last line of his cheerful song, as if confident that America's righteous defence of her rights must triumph.

The June morning was filled with the fragrance of many flowers, and Jan soon left the highway and followed a woodland trail that crossed a number of shallow streams, and made its way up some pleasant slope to again plunge into the cool shade of the forest. The big horse **went on** at a steady, even pace and Joanne, listening to the song of the birds, breathing in the fragrant air and now and then catching a glimpse of a wary fox, a fleeing rabbit, or some other woodland creature, had no thought of being tired until coming out at the edge of a clearing that sloped down to the shores of the Mohawk River Jan drew rein, pulled a big silver watch from his pocket and said:

"We have made good time, and 'tis now high noon. Look toward the river, little maid," and Jan pointed toward the quiet, broad Mohawk that flowed on between the cleared fields and wooded shores, and as Joanne looked in the direction of his pointed finger she exclaimed:

"It's a cabin!" for close down to the water's edge she could see a small log cabin from whose stone chimney rose a faint line of smoke.

Jan nodded smilingly. "'Tis where we'll find a good venison steak, or a well-broiled partridge and some good corn bread, and a drink of cool water. I'll wager you are ready for it," and he smiled over his shoulder at Joanne, who nodded eagerly in response, and with a word to the brown horse they trotted briskly across the rough clearing toward the cabin.

"An old uncle of mine lives here," Jan explained; " he's too old for a soldier, and in times past he has befriended many an Indian, so they do not molest him and he hunts and catches fish and lives in peace and plenty; he will be right glad of news from Albany," and before they reached the cabin Joanne saw an old man standing in the open door shading his eyes with his hand as he watched their approach, and when Jan called out: " Good-morning, Uncle Niel," the old man stepped forward to welcome them, smiling as if well pleased indeed.

" And whose little maid is this? " he asked, as he lifted Joanne from the back of the big horse, smiling upon her so kindly that Joanne at once felt at home with him, and as Jan explained that she was the granddaughter of Madame Clarke of Albany, and that he was taking her to her home in the Mohawk Valley, well up the river toward Fort Stanwix, the old man's face grew very grave and he shook his head.

" 'Tis a dangerous time for such a journey," he said; " the little maid were safer in Albany."

" But I am sent by General Schuyler with messages to General Nicholas Herkimer; and I'm told this small maid has herself brought news of great value to America's cause," said Jan, and he quickly told the story of Red-bird's lost pouch and of the valuable message it had contained, and Uncle Niel's smile returned and he nodded approvingly.

" I have a brace of fine fat partridges ready to broil, and I'll stir up a spider-cake while you feed your horse," he said, " and this little maid can run to the spring for a pitcher of fresh water," and he pointed to an earthenware pitcher that stood on the doorstep and then directed Joanne to the spring which, he said, was near the growth of young birch trees not far from the river, and the little girl started off as she heard Jan say that an hour's rest would be all the time he could spare.

The spring bubbled up close beside the young birches, and kneeling down beside it Joanne drank thirstily, then in a little pool below the spring she bathed her face and hands, and looked about thinking how pleasant a place the little circle of silvery birch trees made. " I'd well like a playhouse here," she whispered, remembering her dolls made of corn-cobs in the far-off hillside cave. Then she went back to the spring, filled the stout gray pitcher, and carried it carefully back to the cabin where Jan was now helping his uncle prepare dinner.

A rough table stood in the center of the room and it was already spread with three tin plates, with a tin cup beside each plate. In the center of the table was a blue earthenware bowl heaped high with wild strawberries and Joanne exclaimed: " Oh, strawberries! " with such delight that Jan laughed aloud, and Uncle Niel smiled with pleasure.

" I picked them this very morning on the slope toward the south. 'Tis early for them, but the season is forward," he said, turning back to the bed of coals over which the fat partridges were broiling, and which were soon on the table together with the crisp spider-cake, a pitcher of milk, and with sugar and thick cream for the fresh strawberries it seemed a feast to the hungry Joanne.

The cabin was so pleasant a place, and Uncle Niel so kind and friendly that Joanne would have well liked to make a longer stay, but as soon as dinner was over Jan again saddled " Sachem," the big horse, and bidding Uncle Niel good-bye they were ready to ride on when the old man said: " Here is a small gift for you, little maid, so that you may remember Uncle Niel," and he handed her a chain of shining beads such as the Indians loved to wear, and that but few white children possessed.

Joanne thanked him delightedly, as she slipped it over her head. She wished that Nancy could see it, and resolved always to keep it. Then at a word from Jan, " Sachem " started forward and in a few minutes they had again entered a forest trail and the little cabin and Uncle Niel were far behind them.

CHAPTER XV

JOANNE AND TALUSHA

As the trail wound now near the river and then across meadow, marsh and woodland, Joanne told her companion of her canoe journey, of Nicholas Campbell, and of the hope she had of meeting Nancy's family on their way to Albany and giving them news of where Nancy could be found; but at this Jan shook his head.

" We'll not be meeting with any who travel on the highway, little maid," he replied, " for the fewer we see until I get to General Herkimer the safer will be the news I carry."

" And will we reach General Herkimer tonight? " asked Joanne, thinking to herself that she would have so many things to tell her mother; and that to see General Herkimer would be another great event among the many that had happened since the game of hide-and-seek she had played with Nancy and Lucy Wagner only a week ago, and she was disappointed when Jan replied:

" I'm not sure when or where I may find General Herkimer, and it may be some days yet. I hope to get news to-night at a settler's house."

Jan was now choosing his path with evident care, and often drew rein and listened as if fearful of the approach of an unseen enemy, as indeed he was, for Jan was a trusted messenger connected with General Schuyler's army, and knew the need of caution.

In the late afternoon the trail led up a hill whose summit they reached just at sunset, and Jan drew rein, dismounted and lifted Joanne from the saddle saying, as he fastened " Sachem's " bridle-rein to the branch of a tree, " Stay you here, little maid, and do not wander out of sight of ' Sachem ' until I return. I'll not be away long, but I must spy out where we are."

Joanne promised, and ventured to reach up and pat " Sachem's " silky brown neck. She had begun to feel a little tired after the long ride, and wondered if Jan would not bring back something for supper.

The hilltop was too thickly wooded for Joanne to see any distance, and as the minutes passed and Jan did not return she remembered how far away she was from her mother; she

thought of Nancy safe in Albany and perhaps
even now acquainted with kind Molly Van Corlear, and Joanne began to feel a little lonely and
homesick, and when she heard a cautious step
behind her she turned smilingly, glad to welcome
Jan, only to find herself looking up into the dark
face of a tall Indian, while just behind him stood
two other braves as if awaiting his word of command.

Before Joanne could speak or call for Jan the
Indian's hand was over her mouth, and his threat-
ening gesture warned the frightened girl to silence. After a muttered whisper to his companions they turned toward " Sachem," who
whinnied anxiously, and began to tug at his bridle-rein, but the alert Indians were both quickly
mounted on " Sachem " and then Joanne's captor
lifted her to the clutching arms of the brave who
was comfortably fixed on the pillion, and who
held Joanne firmly as his companion urged the
horse down the trail.

At the moment when Joanne felt herself being
lifted to " Sachem's " back she screamed loudly,
but her voice was silenced by a swift blow, and
the little girl, stunned and nearly unconscious,
realized nothing of their swift progress down

through the forest until the tired horse stumbled and Joanne and the Indian who held her were suddenly thrown to the ground. Joanne's left arm doubled under her and she screamed in pain.

The other Indian slipped from the saddle and led " Sachem " back; and now the two Indians muttered together, looking at Joanne as she grasped her injured arm and endeavored to keep back her tears; then without a word to her they again mounted and rode away, leaving Joanne alone in the thick dusk of the forest.

At first Joanne was in too great pain to realize what had befallen her. Her face still smarted from the blow she had received, and her arm hurt badly; but in a few moments as the darkness fell about her and she recalled all that had happened she stood up and began to call: " Jan! Jan! Jan! "

The forest echoed her voice, and " Jan! Jan! Jan! " seemed to ring in her ears from every direction, but it was some time before she gave up calling. For the time Joanne entirely forgot Brant's words that courage was her best protection, and fearful of every woodland noise she cowered in the shelter of a big walnut tree, whimpering with pain and terror.

It was an hour or more after the accident when Joanne first heard a clear bird-like whistle that repeated the same note over and over, and told herself that it was some bird that she had never before heard. But as the whistle sounded nearer and nearer, and at last was broken by a queer song, Joanne knew that some human being was approaching and again began to call Jan's name, and adding, " Help me! Help me! " for Joanne had now remembered her silver ring and dared to hope that she might be given aid from some wandering Indian; and suddenly she was sure that some human being was very near her and again she called: " Help me, please help me! " and a moment later a figure moved through the shadowy path and stopped close beside her, and Joanne instantly realized that it was an Indian squaw, and whispered: " Thayendangea," the Indian name of Brant.

There was a muttered exclamation in a hoarse voice, as the squaw came nearer and discovered that a small white girl was crouching close to the trunk of a big tree, evidently hurt and needing aid, and the Indian woman leaned over her but evidently could not understand all that Joanne so eagerly tried to tell her, but she put her arm about the little girl and began talking in a guttural whisper and Joanne was sure she had found a friend as the squaw drew her along the trail and through a narrow path that finally reached a tiny clearing where a little fire, carefully covered with ashes, was still smouldering close beside a wigwam.

The squaw motioned for Joanne to sit down, and kneeling before the fire threw on twigs and bark until it flamed up so that she could see the little girl clearly and Joanne held out her injured arm saying: "It hurts, dreadfully!" and instantly the Indian woman understood and her strong brown fingers clasped Joanne's wrist.

Indian women knew well what to do for such an injury, and Talusha, as Joanne afterward knew to be the squaw's name, quickly prepared smooth splints of wood, tore a strip from the bottom of Joanne's frock, grasped the little girl's arm firmly, and, although Joanne called out at the sudden pain as Talusha set the broken bone, in a few moments the arm was securely bandaged and resting in a sling of soft leather that the squaw contrived from a strip of well-tanned deerskin and Joanne knew that no white woman could have been more tender or more skilful in helping her; and she managed to smile up at the brown face whose sharp eyes were watching her so intently.

Talusha grunted approvingly, and from the wigwam brought a number of soft skins that she spread on the ground, and motioned for Joanne to rest on them. Then she brought a round basket well filled with strawberries that she handed to the little girl and when Joanne began to eat hungrily Talusha nodded, and again vanished, this time in the darkness behind the wigwam; but before Joanne had finished eating the berries the squaw was back again and sitting down near the fire began cutting a strip of venison into tiny bits into a small kettle that she hung over the fire on a forked stick. Joanne watched Talusha as she added bits of a white root to the contents of the kettle, which evidently contained water, and then pieces of green leaves, and very soon an appetizing fragrance drifted toward the hungry girl, so that when the squaw brought her a tin cup filled with broth she drank it eagerly and ate the bits of meat and tender vegetables with such evident satisfaction that a smile for a moment crept about the squaw's mouth and she rested her hand on Joanne's shoulder as if in approval.

"Oh, dear," whispered Joanne, "I wish she could understand what I say," and again the little girl began the story, trying to make her new friend understand that she was on her way up the Mohawk Valley to her own home; but before she had finished Joanne had begun to nod, and the squaw carefully moved the sleepy girl into a comfortable position, and stood for a moment looking down upon her; then she turned back to the smouldering coals, covered them carefully with ashes, and stretched herself beside the sleeping girl.

In the early morning Talusha had been awakened by the patter of rain on the leaves of the forest trees, and by the sound of Joanne's voice moaning as if in pain, and the squaw had carefully lifted her and carried her to the shelter of the wigwam.

Joanne never knew how many days passed as she lay ill and helpless in that tiny wigwam where other dark faces besides that of Talusha came to peer questioningly at the little white girl who wore a silver ring known to be that of the great sachem Brant, whose Indian name, " Thayendangea," the squaw declared the girl had clearly spoken. But it was Talusha who brewed the herb teas that soothed and quieted the fever, and who made nourishing broths that she persuaded Joanne to drink; and when at last the little girl was better and lay outside the wigwam on a couch made of the soft young fir and spruce boughs, it was Talusha who sang a musical bird-like music that Joanne would always remember.

As soon as Joanne could walk, Talusha made preparations to move on. Joanne's broken arm had been skilfully cared for: for many days the squaw had rubbed it with oils known to the Indians for their healing quality, and when the little girl was able to run about the little clearing, always careful to keep close to Talusha, it was as well as before the accident.

But Joanne looked a very different girl from the one who had bidden Grandma Clarke goodbye. Her brown linen dress had disappeared, and her brown stockings and the pretty linen hat had vanished. When she followed Talusha away from the clearing she wore new moccasins, much prettier ones than she had ever before seen, for these were embroidered in bright colored thongs, and her dress was exactly that worn by the young Indian girls: a short skirt of tanned doeskin and a sleeveless tunic of the same, fringed and beaded.

But Joanne was not thinking of these things as she followed Talusha through the forest: she was wondering why the squaw had cut her hair, for no longer did a braid of pretty hair hang nearly to Joanne's waist: the squaw had cut it off close to her head.

The first day Talusha traveled but a short distance, and camped beside the river; and when Joanne saw the wide stretching waters she skipped with delight, and seizing the squaw's arm began to point up-stream and say that in that direction her home lay, where her mother would welcome Talusha. And now for the first time the squaw scowled upon Joanne, pushed her from her, and muttered as if in anger.

"Oh, dear! Whatever will I do? Talusha does not mean to take me home!" Joanne exclaimed, ready to cry with disappointment as she realized that the squaw was probably taking her to some far-off Indian village from which she might never escape, and at that moment Joanne decided that she must escape the squaw's watchful eyes at the earliest moment possible and try and reach her home.

"I can follow the river till I see the bluff where my playhouse is," she resolved, as she lay that night beside Talusha on a moss-covered ledge hidden from the river by a growth of sumac bushes.

CHAPTER XVI

TALUSHA PROVES A FRIEND

But the days passed and still Joanne found no way to carry out her plan. Talusha had taught the little white girl the Indian names for many of the wild flowers, and the roots that the Indians knew were good to eat, as well as how to prepare them for food, and Joanne grew to understand much of what the squaw said; while Talusha, in her turn, knew that Joanne was always pointing up the river and that the little girl was eager to reach some place up the stream where her mother and father lived, and gradually the Indian woman gave up her own plan of taking Joanne to an Indian village on the Canadian frontier where the little captive would grow up as Talusha's daughter, and resolved to restore Joanne to her own family.

To the Indians along the Mohawk in July, 1777, the fortification at the head of the Mohawk River, known as Fort Stanwix, was a place of importance, and Talusha knew that it was held by American soldiers. So when Joanne repeat-

148

edly chattered of her father being a soldier at
Fort Stanwix, it was small wonder that the
squaw became convinced that there was where
Joanne was pleading to be taken, and would say
" Fort Stanwix? " as clearly as Joanne herself,
and then nod and even smile at the little girl until
at last Joanne understood, and realized that she
need no longer fear captivity in an Indian village, and realized that the Mohawk squaw was
her friend.

More than once on their journey Talusha had
avoided bands of Indians, who were journeying
to join forces with the English against the
Americans, fearful lest even Brant's ring might
not be a sufficient protection for the little girl
who the squaw was now determined to deliver
safely at Fort Stanwix; and one hot day toward
the end of July they came out on the right bank
of the Mohawk, and Talusha pointed toward the
fort, within whose walls were then stationed
seven hundred and fifty Continental troops, under the command of Colonel Gansevoort.

As the Indian woman and Joanne stood in the
shade of thickly growing beech trees and looked
toward the fort the little white girl knew that the
time of parting with Talusha was near, and she

tried to thank her for caring for her and bringing her safely to where her soldier father was stationed; and as Joanne looked up into the brown face of the squaw, now so grave and stern, the little girl drew Brant's silver ring from her thumb, and clasping Talusha's hand slipped it upon the squaw's little finger, at the same time saying: " Talusha, dear kind Talusha!"

For a moment the squaw stood silent, her beady eyes fixed on the little girl. Then she began talking eagerly, and Joanne at last understood that Talusha could not keep the silver ring, and that Joanne must never give it away. Then pointing toward the fort the squaw gave Joanne a little push, and the little girl understood that she was to go forward alone; and then, suddenly, Talusha vanished. There was no word of farewell, and tears gathered in Joanne's eyes as she realized that she might never again see the friendly Indian woman who had cared for her so long and brought her to the protection of Fort Stanwix.

Joanne walked slowly forward over the rough ground, and was quickly seen by many watchful eyes, for the Americans at Fort Stanwix in July, 1777, knew that English troops were already on the march to attack them, and the sight of even a small Indian girl, as the watchers believed Joanne to be, boldly approaching the fort might mean danger; so before she reached the walls an armed soldier came toward her, and called out: " Halt! "

Joanne stopped instantly and called back: " If you please, I am Joanne Clarke, and I have journeyed from Albany to see my father! "

" A white girl! " muttered the astonished soldier, for Joanne was so tanned by her out-of-door life that her face and arms were nearly as brown as those of an Indian girl.

" Lieutenant Clarke's little maid? But how ever came you here? " questioned the soldier, as he led the little girl to the entrance of the fort, where a group of soldiers and their wives were gathered, and where one of the women promptly took charge of Joanne, while the soldier who had brought her hurried off to find Lieutenant Clarke and tell him the wonderful news of Joanne's arrival, and in a few moments the little girl's father was listening to the amazing story of all that had befallen her since they last met.

" I had news from your mother yesterday, and she believed you safe and well with your grandmother in Albany. I hope no other news may reach her until she knows you are with me," he said, and Joanne asked eagerly if he knew aught of Lucy Wagner or of Jan Nellis.

"Of Lucy? Why, your mother did mention that Mr. and Mrs. Wagner and Lucy were on their way to Albany. But I have no news of Nellis. 'Tis likely he made his way to General Herkimer, if the Indians did not capture him," replied Lieutenant Clarke, and at that suggestion of capture Joanne exclaimed sorrowfully:

"If he was taken by the Indians I shall never see him again," but her father quickly declared that so clever a woodsman and scout as young Nellis would well know how to take care of himself and escape his enemies. And within a short time Joanne was to hear Jan's story from his own lips and know that for days he had searched for her, and at last believing her a captive of the Indians had given her up.

Listening to her father Joanne was comforted by his confidence that Jan Nellis had escaped capture; and as she told of the Indian woman's kindness as she lay ill in the forest wigwam, and of Talusha's guiding her to Fort Stanwix, it seemed to Lieutenant Clarke that his little

daughter had indeed escaped great danger, and
he resolved that if it were ever possible Talusha
should know of his gratitude.

The families of a number of American soldiers
were sheltered within the walls of Fort Stanwix
in the summer of 1777, and Joanne was willingly
taken in charge by a friendly woman who declared that the little girl would bring good fortune to the fort; and Joanne was glad indeed to
enter a neat room and be given soap, warm water
and a fresh white towel.

" We'll manage a dress for you, little maid,"
the kindly woman assured her; and the next
morning Joanne found a dress of checked cam-
bric ready for her to put on; two of the women
had given skirts of their own from their few
belongings, and had worked by candlelight to
make a dress for the little maid whose safe arrival at Fort Stanwix, after her long journey
from Albany with its many adventures, made
her of interest to everyone within the walls of
the fort, although each and all knew that every
day the menace of an attack by the British and
their Indian allies came nearer.

Red-skinned enemies prowled in the near-by
forests, and the soldiers were constantly on the

alert hoping that General Herkimer and the
militia of Tryon County would reach Fort Stanwix before it was besieged. Lieutenant Clarke
had but little time to be with Joanne, and Mistress Dorshem, who had charge of the little girl,
welcomed her with such evident pleasure that
Joanne soon felt at home with her and listened
eagerly to all Mistress Dorshem told her of the
great happenings that had brought the settlers
from their cabins along the valley of the Mohawk to fight for American liberties.

" Colonel Gansevoort has news that the Continental Congress has determined on a flag, and
I doubt not he would be well pleased if America's
flag flying over Fort Stanwix should meet the
eyes of our enemies," she said one morning as
Joanne was helping clear the table after their
simple morning meal.

" What is the new flag? " Joanne asked, her
thoughts wandering to the stories her mother
had liked so well to tell her of far-off deeds of
valor and of the flags and banners of the knights
of chivalry.

" 'Tis a fine pattern of a flag, little maid;
thirteen stripes, alternate red and white, one for
each of our United States, and the big square

they call the Union in one corner is to be blue, and on this blue field there are thirteen white stars. I'd like well to make such a flag, but there's no fit material in the fort," said Mistress Dorshem, with a little sigh.

" Oh, Mistress Dorshem, my father has a good store of shirts; I heard my mother say they were of stout hand-woven linen; three are blue and three white; would not two of them help toward a flag? And may it not be that there is a red petticoat belonging to some woman in the fort who would gladly give it for the red stripes?" exclaimed Joanne, as she thought how wonderful it would be to help make such a flag.

Mistress Dorshem gazed at the little girl in astonishment, and a radiant smile made her round face glow like a full moon as she clapped her plump hands together.

" And to think I'd not thought of such a thing! 'Tis true for you, little maid, and you the wonder to think of it. Run to your father and bid him give you the stout linen shirts, and I'll wager I'll find the red petticoat. But 'tis every woman in the fort will wish to set a stitch in our flag! Be off with you, like the good girl you are," and the delighted Joanne sped off on her errand.

CHAPTER XVII

THE FLAG OF FORT STANWIX

JOANNE, making her way among groups of soldiers toward the place where her father was stationed, quickly realized that, on this August morning of 1777, some new excitement was stirring; and when a stout officer called out to her: "What are you doing here? Get back to where you belong," the little girl hardly knew what way to turn.

"If you please, I must find my father," she ventured, but the stout officer continued to scowl upon her.

"Do you not know that this very morning the Tory General St. Leger has dared to demand that we surrender this fort to him and his Indian allies, and to threaten us with an immediate attack if we refuse? Be off to whoever has charge of you," and Captain Abraham Swartout was about to go on to more important affairs than talking to a little girl, when Joanne, whose admiring gaze had been fixed on the vivid blue of the captain's coat exclaimed:

" Thirteen white stars on a blue ground! "

" What's that? " asked the captain.

" I was but thinking of the fine blue cloth of your coat, and wishing it could be used for the flag," said Joanne; then, with her best curtsey, she was starting on to find her father, when the captain's clasp on her arm brought her to a standstill.

" ' Flag! ' What's this about a flag? " questioned Captain Swartout, and when Joanne began to tell him what Mistress Dorshem had said he interrupted her eagerly, saying:

" Of course! Of course! We all know that on June 14th, 1777, Congress decided on the design for a flag for the United States, and I would we had one this day that our enemies might see the banner for which we fight."

" And will you give your fine blue coat to help make one? " demanded Joanne, almost dancing in her excitement as she looked up into the puzzled face of the brave officer (whose name was to be long remembered in Mohawk Valley as that of the man who had given his coat toward the making of the first American flag of regulation stars and stripes that had ever floated above a fort in the United States), and then added:

" I know my father will give his white linen
shirts, and Mistress Dorshem doubts not that she
can find a red petticoat for the stripes," and a moment later Joanne was holding the blue coat as
Captain Swartout exclaimed joyfully:

" Take it, take it; and bid the women lose no
time in doing their best to make such a flag,"
and Captain Swartout had slipped off his blue
coat and handed it to the surprised Joanne, and
now smiled upon her with approval. " You'll
be glad to remember this day, little maid," he
said kindly; and Joanne sped off with his
coat, half afraid he might repent and take it
back.

Lieutenant Clarke listened in amazement to
his little daughter's eager story; but he smiled
at the sight of his captain's blue coat, and gave
her the white shirts, and as Joanne turned back
to find Mistress Dorshem, a number of the officers
of the fort gathered about her declaring that if
a flag of the United States could float over Fort
Stanwix it would give new courage to every soldier.

Mistress Dorshem was delighted with Joanne's
success; two other women were in the kitchen,
and one of these immediately seized upon the

JOANNE DID HER BEST TO DRAW A STAR THAT WOULD
PROVE THE RIGHT SIZE FOR THE FLAG

blue coat and, scissors in hand, began to snip off the brass buttons.

"Here, little maid, keep these buttons to remind you of how the flag of Fort Stanwix was made," she said, and Joanne gathered up the shining buttons and strung them on a stout blue cord that Mistress Dorshem drew from her workbag.

"I will always keep them," Joanne declared soberly. "Only I may give one to Nancy Wagner," she added, and thought to herself that if it were ever possible she would like to send a button to kind Molly Van Corlear, and tell her that it was cut from the coat that made the field for the white stars of the flag that was so soon to wave its triumph over injustice.

"Perhaps the little maid can mark out a fine pattern of a star for us," suggested the other woman.

"To be sure she can!" declared Mistress Dorshem. "I have a fine bit of charcoal; she can mark a star on a bit of this roll of birch bark;" and Joanne spread out the silvery bark on one end of the rough table and did her best to draw a star that would prove the right size for the flag; and as she worked Joanne's thoughts traveled off to her own home on the pleasant slope above the Mohawk River, and she earnestly hoped that very soon all the dangers that now threatened the American settlers would be ended, and that she and her father would once more be safely at home.

It was the last day of peace that the fort was to know for days to come. That night the war-whoop of the Indians, led by the terrible Brant, resounded from the near-by forest, and at day-break the next morning the siege of the British and Indians against Fort Stanwix began, and Colonel Gansevoort and his brave soldiers looked anxiously for the arrival of General Nicholas Herkimer and his militia who had been summoned to come to the aid of the little garrison, and who, on August 4th, 1777, had reached Whitestown, only a few miles from Fort Stanwix.

On August 5th, Mistress Dorshem bade Joanne not to leave the cabin; the little girl now began to realize that danger surrounded them on every side, and that Brant's silver ring would be of little protection if the swarming Indians, Tory and British soldiers gained entrance to the fort.

On the morning of August the 6th, 1777, Lieutenant Clarke came hurrying to the Dorshem cabin.

"Colonel Gansevoort wants the flag, if it be indeed a flag you women have managed to make," he said, and it was Joanne who held it up that he might see the fine red stripes, and the blue field of Captain Swartout's coat.

"'Twill serve," he said, with a satisfied smile, and bade Joanne roll it carefully. "And come with me and see it rise over the fort," he added; and Joanne, feeling herself now really a part of the great war, ran along by her father's side until they reached the place where Colonel Gansevoort and Captain Swartout were waiting to receive the flag.

As the flag rose in the hot August air a little breeze came from the river and floated it out triumphantly, and at this a cheer rose in the morning air as the American soldiers saluted the first American flag that had waved over a fort.

"'Tis a good omen," declared a soldier who stood near Joanne, and she wished that she might tell him that she had helped to make that flag; but her father just then bade her hasten back to Mistress Dorshem, and she ran off thinking to herself that as long as the flag waved over the fort it was but little matter who had made it.

Joanne knew but little of the great events that took place on that day at Oriskany, only a few miles distant, when brave General Herkimer was attacked by the hordes of Indian warriors; nor did the little girl know that Colonel Willett with two hundred Americans had left the fort to go to his aid. These brave soldiers attacked and conquered the enemy, the Indians fleeing before them, and the battle of Oriskany proved one of the most important of the American Revolution, and over Fort Stanwix in the face of the beleaguring army of St. Leger floated the American flag.

But it was two weeks later before the defeated British Army began its retreat to Canada, and the Mohawk Valley was saved from the invader; and now Joanne's father would soon be at liberty to return home and Joanne could hardly wait for the time when they would start.

"Will not my mother be surprised when she sees me coming home with Father," she said to Mistress Dorshem as the kindly woman helped the little girl make ready for the journey.

"She will be right thankful, I'll be bound, to

have you safe at home," responded Mistress Dorshem with a smiling nod. " And I'm thinking you may like to carry her a present. What say you to making her a flag of the bits of pieces that were left? "

" Oh, Mistress Dorshem! She would think no present could be better; and may I not begin it this very day? " Joanne replied, and Mistress Dorshem again nodded—Joanne always recalled this kind woman as nodding and smiling at whatever she, Joanne, might say—and brought out the treasured bits of red, white and blue that had been left from the flag, and Joanne was delighted to discover that, by careful " piecing," there would be sufficient material to make a flag large enough to be raised over the cabin; and she eagerly assured Mistress Dorshem that the larger the flag the better pleased her mother would be, and was soon seated by the open window happily at work.

Now and then Joanne would stop to take off the shining steel thimble that Mistress Dorshem had loaned her. It was a thimble that Mistress Dorshem had herself worn when she was a little girl about Joanne's age and when she had lived in far-off Holland, from which country had

come many other of the settlers of Mohawk
Valley.

Joanne resolved to save every tiny bit left from
this second flag and to use the small pieces to
make another flag.

" And perhaps I can find a way to send the
little one to Molly Van Corlear," she thought
hopefully, thinking that such a gift would surely
be welcome to any little girl who was a friend
of General Philip Schuyler.

Joanne's father had secured a canoe for their
journey home, and at last the morning of their
departure was at hand. Mistress Dorshem had
packed the skirt and tunic of deerskin that Joanne had worn on her arrival at Fort Stanwix,
the string of beads that Jan Nellis's old friend
had given her, and the few belongings the little
girl had acquired during her stay in the besieged
fort. These were all tied in a neat package that
could be easily carried in the canoe. Joanne in
the now worn and faded cotton frock, and wearing the beaded moccasins, her short hair standing
out in little curls and waves from beneath the
brim of a clumsy hat which Mistress Dorshem
had made of braided grass, was very different in
appearance from the trig little figure in brown

linen whom Grandma Clarke had started out from Albany.

" My mother will hardly know me, will she, Mistress Dorshem? " Joanne declared smilingly, as she bade the friendly woman good-bye; but Mistress Dorshem, nodding and smiling, declared that Joanne's mother would know her as far as she could see her, and after Joanne had promised to come and visit her good friend whenever it was possible, and when Mistress Dorshem in her turn soberly agreed to come to Joanne's home for a long visit that very autumn, their good-byes were said and Joanne and her father left Fort Stanwix for their journey home.

CHAPTER XVIII

A MYSTERIOUS BASKET

It was sunset when Joanne and her father came in sight of the familiar bluffs beyond which lay their home, and Joanne began happily to call the names of the familiar trees and islands; and Mr. Clarke was, perhaps, even happier than his little daughter to return with her in safety to his cabin home in the wilderness; and when the canoe touched the beach in the well remembered little cove Joanne sprang out before her father could lay down his paddle and raced up the clearing toward the cabin shouting: "Mother! Mother!" But Mr. Clarke was close behind her, and Mrs. Clarke, who had been sitting on the porch, came running to meet them.

"I am almost afraid I'll wake up," she declared, a few moments later, smiling with happiness, as the three of them sat together on the steps of the porch, and talked eagerly of all that had happened since that far-off May when Joanne and Nancy had so unaccountably vanished.

"Where did Lucy hide?" questioned Joanne,

166

leaning against her mother with the resolve that never again would she go away unless her mother went also.

"Lucy? Oh, yes; she was under the porch steps all the while," replied Mrs. Clarke, and she stooped to kiss Joanne's brown cheek, as she remembered those anxious days of the early summer before she received the news that her little daughter was safe in Albany with her Grandmother Clarke.

"And I have supposed you were there all this time," she added; "if I had even imagined you were at Fort Stanwix I should have tried to get there myself."

"It is well you did not know," said Mr. Clarke gravely. "Fort Stanwix was surrounded by St. Leger's English troops, and their Indian allies were on the alert for captives," and again he gratefully thought of how wonderfully his wife and little daughter had been protected from the dangers that encircled them.

As the dusk deepened they went into the cabin, and there was a little feast in the candle-lit kitchen of cool milk and corn bread, and Joanne and her father declared it the best supper they had tasted since leaving home, and they smiled

happily at each other and laughed at the gambols
of a fat gray kitten that jumped into Joanne's
lap as soon as she was seated at the table, and
would have jumped on the table had not the little girl held it firmly.

When Mrs. Clarke discovered that Joanne's
beautiful hair had been cut short she exclaimed
in dismay:

" Joanne! What ever happened to your beautiful hair? "

Joanne put up her hand and smoothed back
the unruly waves of short hair as she answered:

" I s'pose Talusha must have cut it off when I
was sick in the wigwam. Anyway, when I woke
up one day it was gone," and the little girl began
to tell of all the kindness the Indian woman had
shown her on that journey through the forest.
" I wish I could see Talusha again," she concluded thoughtfully.

" Perhaps you will, my dear. Who knows but
what she may come and visit us; and if she does
we will give her a warm welcome," replied Mrs.
Clarke.

That night as Joanne lay in her own comfortable bed, the soft summer air stirring the linen

curtains of her open windows, the contented purr of the gray kitten, comfortably established on the foot of her bed, sounding like a friendly welcome, Joanne drew a little sigh of complete happiness.

" I'm home again, and Father is home safe, and we are both going to stay here, and to-morrow I'll go to the cave and fix it all up," and with these pleasant thoughts she drifted into sleep.

She was up at an early hour the next morning, and looked admiringly at the pile of neat underclothing, the homespun linen dress, and a pair of soft, low moccasins that her mother had ready for her to put on.

" I guess I used to think clothes just grew," Joanne whispered as she slipped into the fresh garments, her thoughts going back to the few worn and clumsy pieces of clothing that was all Mistress Dorshem could provide for her at the fort; henceforth Joanne had a new satisfaction and pleasure in the clean simple dresses that her mother made for her.

There was so much to tell Mother about Albany; about Red-bird and the pouch with its important message that Joanne had carried to General Philip Schuyler.

"And, Mother, he has little daughters no older than I am; and he said I was brave and faithful to bring the pouch to him as quickly as I could! And, oh, Mother, a little girl told me the way to his house; the prettiest little girl in Albany!" Joanne declared eagerly; and Mrs. Clarke was as eager to hear the story as Joanne was to tell of friendly Molly Van Corlear's help to a little maid of Mohawk Valley.

Indeed there was so much to talk about that it was nearly noon before Joanne remembered the wonderful flag she had made at Fort Stanwix, and ran to open the bundle and bring it for her mother to admire.

"I made every stitch of it, Mother dear, from the pieces left from the big flag; and the white stripes and stars are made of Father's linen shirts, and the red stripes are the petticoat of a neighbor of kind Mistress Dorshem's, and the blue is the coat of Captain Abraham Swartout," said Joanne as her mother held up the flag and looked at it admiringly.

"We will always keep this, Joanne," she said gravely, "and remember that it stands for Justice."

"We will have a liberty pole of our own,"

declared Mr. Clarke, standing in the open doorway. "I'll cut the finest pine in our woodland
and set it up in the clearing, and every morning
Joanne shall send the flag to the top of the pole
and at sunset she shall lower it."

Joanne gave her usual little skip of delight at
so pleasant a prospect. "Will you not cut the
pine tree to-day, Father?" she asked, and Mr.
Clarke smilingly agreed that he would start at
once in search of a pine tall enough for a fine
liberty pole, such as loyal Americans were set-
ting up in all the thirteen states that were fighting for their rights.

As Joanne took out the treasured bits of red,
white and blue and put them in a covered basket
she suddenly exclaimed:

"Mother! I am going to make two more flags!
One for Grandmother Clarke and one for Molly
Van Corlear! Do you not think there may be
a chance for me to send them to Albany before
winter comes?"

"Very likely, my dear; messengers from Fort
Stanwix and the frontier may be traveling to
Albany, and if they chance to come this way
would take the little flags for you," replied Mrs.
Clarke; and Joanne now declared that she must

run to the bluff and find out if her treasures were safe in the long-forsaken playhouse.

"And will you not come with me, Mother?" she pleaded.

"Indeed I will. You are not to be out of our sight again, Joanne, until the English are driven home and the Indians are taught better manners," replied Mrs. Clarke, and they walked across the clearing and up the slope, and in a few moments Joanne was at the entrance to the cave and was about to enter when she started back exclaiming:

"Mother, did you put a basket here?"

"Why, of course not! Let me see," and Mrs. Clarke kneeled beside her little daughter and peered into the cave, and with a little exclamation of surprise drew out a basket shaped like a canoe, and beautifully made of fragrant wild grass and delicate thongs of deerskin brightly colored, and coiled about in the basket lay a long braid of silky brown hair.

"Oh, Mother! Mother! Talusha must have brought this and left it here for me! Do you suppose she is near? Talusha! Talusha!" called Joanne at the top of her voice, and for a brief moment the little girl and her mother both listened as if expecting the Indian woman to appear, but there was no response, and at last Joanne decided that her mother must be right in saying that very likely Talusha had left the basket there weeks earlier.

"But how did she ever know it was my playhouse? I don't see how anyone could know," questioned the puzzled girl; but that was a question that Mrs. Clarke could not answer, and Joanne was never to know the whole story of Talusha's discovery of the Clarke cabin and of the playhouse in the cave.

"Will we take the basket home?" asked Joanne, when she had made sure that the corncob dolls were safe, and resolved to make them into a regiment of soldiers.

"Yes, indeed. Your Talusha evidently left it as a gift for you, and I mean to keep this poor braid!" replied her mother, holding up the crinkly braid of Joanne's hair. As they started back toward the cabin, Joanne was quiet as they walked through the grass that was now turning a little brown and rustled beneath their steps. The little girl was thinking of Talusha wandering alone through the forest searching for the home of the little girl she had so wonderfully befriended; and as they neared the cabin she said soberly:

"I love Talusha! I wish I could see her."

"Perhaps you will, dear child. I wish I might see her and thank her for caring for you and taking you to your father," said Mrs. Clarke, and then added: "To-day we are going to have a real feast. You do not know what a farmer I am, Joanne! I have as good a crop of corn as your father himself could have raised. I have onions and beans, cabbage and potatoes, and peas and turnips. And I have a fat young rooster roasting this minute in the brick oven! And, though I have no white flour to make a cake, I mean to have a potato pudding with cream sauce!"

"Oh, Mother! Will dinner soon be ready?" asked Joanne, quite sure that she had never been so hungry before in all her life.

Mrs. Clarke laughed delightedly as they ran up the cabin steps.

"You will have to help, Joanne. Here are the peas for you to shell," she continued, as the little girl set down her beautiful basket in the sitting-room and followed her mother into the kitchen.

" I'll get my apron," said Joanne, running to the corner of the kitchen where hung a gingham apron that had been awaiting its small owner all through the summer months.

She had just seated herself on the back door-step with the basket of peas beside her when she heard the sound of voices and looked up to see her father and a tall young man coming down the path from the forest; the young man was leading a horse and Joanne began to wonder if she was really seeing straight, for surely that young man looked exactly like Jan Nellis, and the horse must be the very same horse on which she had so happily left Albany.

But she had not quite made sure when the young man waved his cap gaily and called:

" Well, little maid! I had a fine search for you," and Joanne jumped up and ran to meet him, calling out:

" Jan! Jan! And you were not killed or scalped or captured, were you, after all! "

" We have a fine dinner," Joanne announced a little later on, after Jan had spoken with Mrs. Clarke and told her of his search for Joanne, and as the young man took his seat at the well-spread table he was quite sure the little girl was right and that it was a feast indeed. He was eager to hear of Joanne's adventures with the Indian woman, and when the little girl told of finding the basket that morning in the cave, Jan promptly declared that he believed Talusha was not far away.

"You may see the squaw any day," he said, smiling at Joanne's eager look.

"She isn't a squaw, she's my friend," Joanne responded soberly.

CHAPTER XIX

A CELEBRATION IS PLANNED

JAN told the Clarkes that he was now journeying back to his home in Albany, but he was easily persuaded to remain for a week at the Clarkes' pleasant cabin, and promised the delighted Joanne that he would carry her gifts and safely deliver them to Molly Van Corlear and to Madame Clarke in Albany; and on the day after his arrival Joanne brought her work-basket to the front porch of the cabin, seated herself comfortably on the upper step, and with the gray kitten jumping about her, began happily to work on the small flags.

Her cheeks were still deeply brown from her weeks in the summer sunshine, and her short brown hair waved about her face as she bent over her sewing; and Mrs. Clarke, looking at her little daughter, seemed to see also another little girl with a fairer skin and a long braid of hair, the Joanne of the previous spring.

Joanne had been at work only a short time

when she heard the sound of voices, the rattle of chains and her father's call to the horses that were drawing the pine tree for the liberty pole to the clearing, and in a few moments the sturdy gray horse belonging to the Clarkes harnessed with the high-spirited " Sachem " came in sight and behind them trailed the long pole.

" Joanne," called her father, " tell your mother to come and help us decide where the pole shall stand; " but at that moment Mrs. Clarke appeared in the open doorway, and Joanne put aside her work to run beside her mother down the clearing to where her father and Jan were waiting.

" I wish it could be set up on the bluff near my playhouse," said Joanne, thinking to herself that then all travelers along the Mohawk would be sure to see the flag; but it was finally decided that the liberty pole should be placed half-way between the cabin and the shore, and that night it stood as firmly in place as if it had indeed grown there; but the swinging lines, and small blocks for raising the flag, that Jan had cleverly contrived, showed it to be indeed a flagstaff.

" Let us do our best to have a fine flag-raising," suggested Jan Nellis, with his pleasant smile. "September the 6th is but a few days distant, and 'tis the birthday of young Lafayette, who is giving such aid to our American Army. Shall we not raise the flag for the first time on his birthday, in honor of the brave Frenchman?"

" 'Tis a fine idea; and I could wish there were neighbors at hand to help us with such a celebration," replied Mr. Clarke.

"But the Eatons are in their cabin. They did not leave home after all. Mrs. Eaton and her widowed sister have often walked the two miles between our cabins to help me with my garden," said Mrs. Clarke, "and 'tis an easy walk; one of us can go over this very night and bid them come. Grandpa Eaton is well able to walk the distance."

" ' Sachem ' will carry me over the trail in no time," said Jan, and while Mr. Clarke told him the location of the Eatons' cabin the young man slipped the saddle on the brown horse, and was speedily galloping down the woodland trail.

" 'Twill be a holiday for the Eatons to come for such a sight as the raising of an American flag in the Mohawk Valley," said Mrs. Clarke; "we'll do our best for them to enjoy the day.

I'll give them an excellent dinner for one thing," she concluded laughingly, " and Grandpa Eaton shall make a speech."

" I'm going down to my playhouse," said Joanne, and promising to come back before the sun sank behind the distant forest, she ran off toward the bluff. Before entering the cave Joanne seated herself in her usual resting-place and looked down at the peaceful waters of the Mohawk, that now mirrored the vivid colors of the approaching sunset. Her thoughts traveled down the wide stream over which she and Nancy had journeyed with the friendly scout, and she wished that Nancy and Lucy were in their own home, and could come to the flag-raising in Lafayette's honor.

It was the first day of September, and the summer's warmth still lingered; there was no air stirring, but suddenly Joanne realized that the tall grass just beyond the entrance to the cave was swaying as if pushed aside by some moving creature, and Joanne, looking steadily toward it, was for a moment frightened and tempted to flee homeward; but the grass ceased to move, and Joanne assured herself that some young fox, or perhaps a rabbit, was the cause of her fear.

" Or maybe it was my fairy," she thought, smiling as she entered the cave, but her first step brought her to a standstill, and she exclaimed aloud, for she had nearly stumbled over another basket; and as she picked it up and stepped outside Joanne called eagerly: " Talusha! Talusha! " for she now felt sure that the Indian woman had been lurking behind the swaying grass.

But there was no response to her call, and Joanne now looked at the basket, and saw that it was well filled with big ripe blackberries, so fresh that they must have been recently gathered. This basket had evidently been hastily made; it was of silvery birch-bark, and its square corners were fastened with stout grass.

" Oh, Talusha! I do wish you wouldn't hide! " said Joanne pleadingly, as she stood in front of the cave, carefully holding the basket that was so strong a proof that the Indian woman was not far away. But Joanne now realized that the sun was disappearing behind the dark line of the forest, and reluctantly turned toward home. The more she thought of Talusha the more eager she was to discover her and bring her to the cabin, and before she reached the steps she was calling:

"Mother! Father!" so earnestly that Mr. and Mrs. Clarke came running to meet her, half afraid some harm had befallen her.

"See!" Joanne exclaimed, holding out the basket. "And the grass moved, and I know Talusha must have seen me. Do you not think we can find her, Father?" and Joanne looked up with so pleading a look that her father answered quickly:

"We must let Talusha know that she will be welcome. Take out the berries and fill the basket with food; and have you not something, Joanne, that Talusha will remember that you can put in the basket and we will then carry it back to the cave."

"My silver ring!" exclaimed the little girl. " I wanted to give it to her but she would not take it. Perhaps she will now!"

"Nothing could be better," declared Mr. Clarke; and Joanne hurried to empty the fine berries into a pewter bowl, and Mrs. Clarke filled the birch-bark basket with cold chicken, freshly baked corn bread and butter and a glass of wild grape jelly.

"We will all go to the cave with the basket," said Mr. Clarke; "then, if she really is hiding

near by, Talusha will see that the whole family
are friendly toward her."

But it was Joanne who set the basket just
within the entrance to the cave, and then drew
from her thumb the silver ring Brant had given
her on that May day that now seemed so long
ago, and put it carefully where anyone stooping
over the basket would be sure to see it.

"Do you suppose Talusha will come back to-
morrow and wait here for me?" Joanne asked
eagerly, as clasping her mother's hand they
turned toward home.

"I am afraid it may not be as easy to convince
her as you hope, Joanne. But if she does not let
you see her after she finds your ring we will think
up some other plan to convince her that we are
her friends," responded Mr. Clarke.

"And may she not live with us always?"
urged Joanne.

"As long as she pleases to stay," replied her
mother, smiling down at Joanne's eager face.

Jan was at the cabin on their return, and said
that the Eatons were greatly pleased with the
news of the safe return of Joanne and her father.

"I told them the story of the Battle of Oriskany, where brave Herkimer received his death

wound, and old Mr. Eaton declared it was a
battle that would some day be known as one of
the bravest in American history; and the family
will all come to the flag-raising," he said, and
added smilingly: "I told them of the flag that
floats over Fort Stanwix, and that this little maid
had a hand in making it," and he nodded toward
Joanne.

But the little girl was not listening to the con-
versation: she was looking toward the bluff, her
thoughts fixed on Talusha, wondering if the Indian woman might not at that very moment be
eating the food they had carried to the cave and
perhaps even wearing the silver ring, and she
suddenly jumped up declaring that she wanted
to go back to the playhouse.

"I'm sure Talusha is there!" she said.

But Mrs. Clarke convinced her that it would
be best to wait until morning, and Joanne, followed by the gray kitten, went to her own room
and prepared for bed.

"I'll go to the cave the very first thing to-
morrow morning," she confided to the gray
kitten, who mewed faintly as if to agree with its
small mistress.

But the next morning a pouring rain drenched

grass and woodland, the wind swept it fiercely against the cabin, and thrashed the branches of the trees so that they creaked and moaned with every fresh gust, and even Joanne admitted that she must not venture to the bluff.

" Indians know well how to find shelter in such a storm," said Jan, who was seated near one of the kitchen windows using his pocket-knife to carve a doll's head from a block of soft pine.

" Perhaps she may come to the cabin," suggested Joanne, as she watched the young man's clever fingers, and wondered for whom the doll was being made.

" It may be," he replied, " but you can work on your flags since you must stay indoors," and Joanne brought her work-basket and drew out her own steel thimble and was soon stitching the red and white stripes neatly together, and telling Jan of the care Talusha had so tenderly given her when she lay ill in the forest wigwam. " And I can't bear to think of her wandering about in storms," concluded the little girl.

" Joanne, don't jump up or call," said Jan in a whisper, " but I think Talusha is peering in the window at us. I'm not sure, only that it is an Indian, perhaps a hostile one! "

But before his sentence was finished the work-basket was on the floor and Joanne had darted across the room and pulled open the door, calling " Talusha! Talusha! " as she rushed out into the storm, and the amazed Indian woman, for it was indeed Talusha, felt herself suddenly clasped by a wind-blown little figure who began to draw her toward the cabin door exclaiming over and over: " Dear Talusha, dear, good Talusha, come in out of the storm. You are to live with us forever; " and although the squaw could not understand the words she readily understood the delight and eagerness of Joanne's welcoming clasp, and permitted the little girl to draw her through the open door into the kitchen.

CHAPTER XX

TALUSHA

JOANNE was eager that Talusha should realize that she had been hoping to see her again; and that a little white girl could prove as kind and thoughtful as Talusha had been during those long summer days when Joanne lay helpless in the wigwam of the Indian woman.

She led Talusha about the cabin, explaining the use of any article in which the Indian woman showed interest, and declared that Talusha was to sleep in her room.

Mrs. Clarke agreed, and smiled so kindly upon this unexpected visitor that Talusha's grim face grew less solemn and she found herself smiling in response. But she shook her head and grunted disapprovingly at the idea of sleeping in Joanne's bed; and that night carried a blanket to the porch and made her new friends understand that henceforth during her visit at the cabin the porch was to be her sleeping quarters.

" 'Twill do well enough through these pleasant

autumn nights; and it is full likely she will be off to her own tribe before really cold weather sets in," said Mrs. Clarke, as she came to Joanne's chamber to bid her little daughter good-night. But at her mother's suggestion that Talusha would not remain, that the Clarkes' home would not always be that of the Indian woman, Joanne sat up in bed, looking as if she were about to cry, and exclaimed:

"Mother! Talusha can't go away. I want her to live here! Mother! Don't you want her to stay with us always?" and Joanne's gray eyes were so earnest and beseeching that Mrs. Clarke realized her little daughter's gratitude and affection for the Indian woman was sincere. She resolved to do all that seemed possible to persuade Talusha to remain, and quickly responded:

"We will all do everything we can to make Talusha contented, but she has proven her affection for you, Joanne, and is now sure of your safety, and 'twill be but natural that she, too, should want to go to her own people."

But Joanne was not so easily consoled; at the possibility, even, that Talusha might not want to remain, except for a visit, she began to recall all the delights of the Indian woman's companionship; to remember the crooning songs, the bird-calls, the imitating of the " talk " of woodland animals with which Talusha had so cleverly entertained her small companion as they wandered through the forest or camped beside some woodland stream. Long after her mother had said " Good-night, and pleasant dreams," Joanne lay awake thinking of plans to keep Talusha happy and contented at the cabin. " If she thought I needed her I know she would stay forever," she decided and resolved to make the Indian woman realize that the little white girl still depended upon her. " I know what I'll do. I'll get lost, and Talusha will find me; and I'll make her believe that I might get lost again and *never* be found if she wasn't here to search for me." And believing she had discovered the right way to keep Talusha at the cabin Joanne went happily to sleep.

The next morning was clear and warm, and Joanne was up at an early hour and out on the porch to make sure that her friend had not vanished during the night. Talusha was awake and pointed toward the river, easily making the little girl understand that she was ready for a dip in the cool water. Joanne eagerly agreed, darting back to her room for a couple of the home-made towels, and then running swiftly after Talusha, and in a few moments they were both swimming in the smooth waters of the cove, coming back to the cabin with excellent appetites for the hot porridge and cream, the well cooked bacon and eggs, and the corn bread.

It was Joanne who persuaded Talusha to sit beside her at the kitchen table, and who kept her plate filled. Mr. and Mrs. Clarke and Jan were all careful not to notice Talusha, beyond an occasional friendly nod or word, and she was well used to eating with the little white girl. Before the meal was over Talusha was doing her best to use knife, fork and spoon in the same way that the others did; and, as no one smiled at her broken English, she would repeat Joanne's words over questioningly, and the little girl would try to explain their meaning.

The day that followed was a busy and happy day for Joanne. She and Talusha had no difficulty in understanding each other; for the little girl during their weeks together had learned the meaning of many Indian names, and had taught Talusha a number of English words, and, beside these, a look or a sign meant certain things to each of them. Joanne was sure there could not be a better playmate than the Indian woman who knew so much about birds and rabbits, squirrels, bees and all the wild creatures of the fields and woods; and before the day was over Joanne had given up her plan of losing herself in order that Talusha might rescue her; for the little girl was now sure that Talusha would not want to wholly desert her; that, even if she went to her own people, she would return to the little white girl whose life she had saved.

Jan gave the wooden doll to Joanne, and she and Talusha quickly decided that it should be an Indian doll, and taking it to Joanne's playhouse on the bluff they worked happily making the wooden figure into a brown-faced image of a young Indian.

Talusha stained its face with the juices of crushed walnut bark; she made its eyes black with charcoal, and its lips were reddened with bittersweet. It was provided with a thick braid of brown moss that Talusha fastened skilfully to the wooden head with a thread-like thong which she cut from the top of her own moccasin. Then, from the bundle that she always carried, Talusha produced a roll of finely tanned skin and with a few strokes of the sharp knife, that she wore in a stout leathern sheath, shaped a tunic which 'she speedily sewed together with thongs.

Joanne watched her eagerly, and when the Indian woman drew out a store of bright feathers and shining beads and, with a smiling nod at Joanne's expression of delight, began to skilfully embroider the neck and then the skirt of the doll's tunic the little girl jumped about declaring the Indian doll would be the finest doll in all the Mohawk Valley.

And when she carried it to the cabin Mr. and Mrs. Clarke quite agreed with her; for the doll wore the finest of moccasins, the richest of tunics; on its head was a tiny circlet of feathers, and its stiff wooden arms held a drawn bow, while a quiver filled with feather-tipped arrows hung at its side.

Jan Nellis said it ought to be sent to Lafayette as a birthday present; but Joanne promptly announced that she meant to keep it forever. " Because Talusha made it for me," she exclaimed, clasping Talusha's brown hand.

And Joanne did indeed keep this Indian doll until she was an old woman, and told its history to many younger friends, and always declared it to be one of her most valued possessions; but now her thoughts fled to Nancy and Lucy Wagner, and she wished they might be with her to admire this wonderful doll as well as to be present at the raising of the American Flag which was to be on the following day.

CHAPTER XXI

SURPRISES

THE day for the raising of the flag proved clear and sunny, and at an early hour Joanne was out on the porch looking across the clearing for the first sight of the expected guests. Talusha hovered close behind the little girl; and Mrs. Clarke, looking from the cabin window, smiled as she called the attention of her husband to their little daughter and the brown-faced Indian woman whose watchful glance seemed to surround and protect her companion.

" I am never anxious about Joanne now," said Mrs. Clarke, " for Talusha never seems to lose sight of her, and I know will protect her from any possible danger. I hope she means to stay with us."

" Of course she does," declared Mr. Clarke. " She and Joanne are building a wigwam just at the edge of the forest where, Joanne tells me, Talusha intends to live, although when the winter sets in she may be glad to come to the

194

cabin. With Brant's savages wandering through the valley we can have no better protection than the fact that Talusha is a part of our household. I am thankful that she is so surely Joanne's friend."

Talusha had quickly realized how genuine a welcome she had received, and it was plain to everyone that now her only thought was to be near to Joanne. During the weeks when the little white girl had lain sick and helpless, wholly dependent upon her care and kindness, the squaw's heart had centered upon her; and she had left her at the fort only because she believed Joanne would be happier with her own people; nevertheless, Talusha had resolved to make sure that all was well with the girl, and so had sought out and discovered the Clarkes' cabin where she had been so warmly welcomed; and as the days passed with Joanne's eagerness to teach her the English names of all that surrounded her, with the little girl running after her, the warm little hand clasping her own and the clear gray eyes resting trustfully on hers, Talusha grew less and less inclined to go back to her wandering life. She liked the abundance of good food that Mrs. Clarke set before her, she liked the friendly words that greeted her, and on the day before the time set for the flag-raising she had led Joanne to a sunny little opening at the edge of the woodland, near where Joanne, Nancy and Lucy had played hide-and-seek, and had easily made the little girl understand her wish to build a wigwam, and Joanne had worked sturdily beside the squaw, dragging the stout birch saplings that Talusha carefully selected and chopped down, and that would form the framework for the wigwam, and the little girl made many plans for the comfort of her Indian friend, promising Talusha that Mrs. Clarke would bestow upon her all the blankets she wanted; a statement that the squaw seemed to readily understand as she nodded her approval with grunts and smiles.

The Eatons arrived in good season, and were warmly welcomed, Grandpa Eaton insisting that Joanne should promptly tell him the story of her journey to Albany, and describe her meeting with General Philip Schuyler, which the little girl was quite ready to do, and, after she had drawn a comfortable chair to the porch for old Mr. Eaton to rest in, she recounted her adventures, the old man listening with evident interest, and when she told of the making of the American flag that now floated over Fort Stanwix, he exclaimed:

"A great day for Mohawk Valley and for the American cause. When the British soldiers saw that flag they must have known it would never be lowered; and this is a proud day, little maid, when on the birthday of the gallant Lafayette we raise the American flag in his honor, a flag made by a little maid of Mohawk Valley."

As the Clarkes and their neighbors and Jan Nellis seated themselves at the dinner table Joanne exclaimed:

"Where is Talusha? I have not seen her since I ran to meet Mrs. Eaton. I must find her!" and before anyone could reply the little girl was out of doors calling the squaw's name; and when no answer came the little girl stood looking off toward the river, puzzled and unhappy, fearful that the Indian woman might have really decided to go back to her own people, and at this thought tears came to Joanne's eyes.

"It will spoil everything if Talusha goes away," she thought unhappily, and at that moment a light touch on her shoulder made her turn quickly to find the Indian woman beside her.

"Oh, Talusha!" and now Joanne smiled with

delight, making the squaw understand that she must come and share the feast prepared for the flag-raising.

As Joanne, holding the squaw fast by the hand, returned to the kitchen the visitors looked at them in evident amazement, while Grandpa Eaton muttered: "Bless my soul! Bless my soul!" as if too surprised at the presence of a friendly Mohawk squaw to remember that, before the outbreak of war, the Mohawk Indians had often proven themselves not unfriendly toward the settlers.

But it was to prove a day of surprises, for Talusha had just been helped to a generous supply of broiled venison, corn, peas and jelly, when the entire party were startled by loud calls from the clearing, and Mr. Clarke, Jan Nellis and Joanne all hurried to the porch half fearing the calls might be those of an approaching enemy.

"Nancy! Lucy!" shouted Joanne with a rush down the steps and across the clearing to meet the little party that were hastening toward the cabin; for Mr. Wagner and his wife and children had journeyed up from Albany with the boats sent to supply Fort Stanwix with supplies, and had now paddled over from their own home to visit their friends.

Nancy was wearing one of the pretty dresses that Joanne's grandmother had given her, and as the little girls talked eagerly together of the wonderful happenings of the past summer Nancy said:

" Your grandma sent you a fine package, Joanne; and my father brought it over this morning. She sent you the pretty dresses, and the slippers and the things that you would have had if you had stayed in Albany!"

But Joanne was too eager for news of Molly Van Corlear, of General Philip Schuyler, and in her turn to tell of her stay at the besieged fort, and of Talusha's coming to live with the Clarkes, to think much about the package. It was not until the following day that the package was opened and its contents examined and admired.

" And all the things that happened to us, Nancy, happened because Lucy hid away from us," said Joanne, as the three little girls walked together toward Joanne's playhouse, with Talusha sauntering behind them.

Lucy smiled as if she thought Joanne meant to praise her for some clever accomplishment.

" Yes," she answered, with evident satisfaction, " I guess *I* am the one General Schuyler ought to praise instead of Joanne! "

" Why, Lucy Mehitable Wagner! " exclaimed Nancy. " *You* were to blame for Joanne and I getting lost! "

Lucy nodded. " I know it! And if you hadn't been lost Red-bird would not have found you and carried you off, and then General Schuyler would not have had that important news in the letter Joanne carried to him, the news that made all the little girls in Albany say they wished they could have seen you, Joanne. They all call you ' The Little Maid of Mohawk Valley.' "

" Did you see Molly Van Corlear, and did she call me that? " Joanne asked eagerly, and Nancy quickly responded:

" Yes, Joanne, and she bade me say she would not forget you; but Lucy was to blame and she knows she was, and she need not talk in so silly a manner. If she does I shall tell Mother," and Nancy looked reprovingly at her small sister. But Lucy smiled confidently, and slipped back to walk beside Talusha, while Joanne told Nancy of the flags she had made for her Grandmother Clarke and for Molly Van Corlear.

" Jan Nellis is to take them. He starts early to-morrow for Albany," she said; " and they are so small they can easily be carried in his pocket."

The girls were now at the cave, and while Lucy explored it, and Talusha seated herself near its entrance, Nancy and Joanne continued to talk of the exciting events of the summer, and Nancy noticed the silver ring, that Talusha had insisted Joanne should continue to wear.

" Do you remember what Brant said when he gave it to me?" Joanne asked, adding quickly, " He said, ' Courage is your best protection.' I used to think of it, Nancy, when I was at Fort Stanwix because it was the courage of the American soldiers that made them win the battle of Oriskany."

Before Nancy could answer Jan Nellis came to call them to the clearing, where the Wagners, the Eatons and Mr. and Mrs. Clarke were gathered about the liberty pole.

Grandpa Eaton made the promised speech, telling of the brave young Lafayette who had so generously offered his services to the cause of American liberties; he spoke of the men of Mohawk Valley who had so recently proven their loyalty and courage in driving the British and their Indian allies from the valley, and then drawing his flute from his pocket he began to play " Yankee Doodle "; and as the gay music sounded on the quiet September air, Jan Nellis attached the flag to the cords that ran to the top of the liberty pole and handed them to Joanne and in a moment the " Stars and Stripes " slid smoothly to the top of the flagstaff, caught the little drifting breeze from the river and floated above the heads of the little group of loyal Americans.

Grandpa Eaton waved his flute and shouted: " Three cheers for our flag! " and the cheers were given with a will.

" And three cheers for Lafayette," said Jan; and then they cheered Washington, and last of all the brave Nicholas Herkimer, the hero of Oriskany, who, mortally wounded, directed the battle until success was assured.

Then Grandpa Eaton again played the gay measure of the tune that was always to recall to Americans the struggles and triumphs of the courageous settlers, and the little party of neighbors and friends made their way back to the porch.

But Talusha stood looking up at the banner

that floated above the cabin and tree-tops; looking up the Indian woman understood but vaguely all that this symbol might mean. As the British and their Indian allies fled from Fort Stanwix Talusha had seen this starry banner mounted above British flags; she knew, therefore, that it meant that the Americans were stronger than their foes. She had seen Joanne happily at work on tiny flags to send as gifts sure to be valued, and now she had watched this flag raised with music and cheers, and she firmly believed it would henceforth prove a protection against all dangers.

Joanne left her friends on the porch and came running across the clearing, and clasping Talusha's hand the two friends, the Indian woman and the little maid of Mohawk Valley looked up at the flag, and Joanne, almost unconsciously, began to hum the air that Grandpa Eaton had played a little earlier.

END